MW00961581

"Rick Kavanaugh is known as a man of prayer and of having led churches where he has pastored into an appreciation for, and the practice of, deeper prayer. This book will assist the serious student of prayer in the discovery and development of a vibrant prayer life as Pastor Rick applies his considerable skill as a teacher to this critical topic for every fully devoted follower of the Master. I commend this book to you."

—HC Wilson,
General Superintendent Emeritus
The Wesleyan Church

" Rick captures the essence of Faith in his latest book. I have read and heard sermons my entire life regarding the Fig Tree, but the divine illumination regarding the Root and the Leaves left me with a completely new and refreshing perspective on how we pray and confess, as well as face adversity in our lives. *Believing at the Root* is spot on. Get your copy today, and start a new journey in your faith walk."

—Roy Morgan
Premier Productions | www.PremierProductions.com

"Though billed as a book on prayer; I found this to be a study on living a faith-filled life in the midst of the complexities of our day-to-day walk with Christ. It is written by a man who is a deep student of the Word yet the profound contribution of the book is watching Rev Kavanaugh pursuing God at all costs. This is a shining light of hope to all who will read this work. Pastor Rick will not just explain the text but he will take us by the hand and guide us through the trials and travails of prayer, all the while pointing to the One who answers our cries for help. He is a pastor, teacher and a fellow traveler all at the same time."

—Dr. David Smith
Professor of New Testament
Indiana Wesleyan University

"I'm excited to recommend Rick Kavanaugh's latest book. I've known Rick for years and he really lives what he preaches. That's why I am grateful that he is making his insights available beyond his effective ministry to his local church. This book will be a tremendous help as you embrace the adventure of walking with God in faith."

—Mark Gorveatte
Author of *Lead Like Wesley*

Believing At The Root

Believing At The Root

Learning To Bridge The Gap Between God's Reality And Your Experience

Rick Kavanaugh

It was on the anvil of trial and error that most of the principles in this book were hammered out. I am indebted to the congregation in Presque Isle, Maine, who for many years was patient and gracious with me as I stumbled along, trying to understand how to walk in the Spirit. I made many mistakes, but their encouragement, support, prayer and passion for Christ always kept me going. I owe so much to them and will always be thankful I was given the privilege of serving in that part of God's Kingdom. A project like this is never completed in isolation. There were several who have stepped into the process. I want to thank Phil Halvorson, Heidi Samuel, Rich Gufastason and Jerry Klinger for helping with the editing process. Your extra sets of eyes saved me a lot of embarrassing mistakes. I am also thankful to Mark Gorveatte for his encouraging and sage advice. Your insights have been a great help in getting me across the finish line.

Contents:

Introduction

In 1992 my life long friend and prayer partner, Phil Halvorson, and I were sitting at a table in Hyde Park Vermont, listening to a pastor give a morning devotional. We were there for the week to receive training in Scriptural counseling. I don't remember anything about the seminar training that morning, but I will never forget that fifteen-minute devotional. I remember looking at Phil and saying, "If what this guy is saying is true, this could change our lives." And it did. I took his lesson to heart and applied it to my life. I have studied and lived out this principle over the last 25 years. I am thankful to God and Dr. Gary Durham for sharing that devotional with us. His talk provided the seeds from which this study has evolved over the years. I hope it will be as life changing to you as it has been to me.

The story begins in Mark, chapter 11. The setting is Passover week, the time of Jesus' triumphal entry into Jerusalem. Mark leads into the story in verse 11. "Jesus entered Jerusalem and came into the temple; and after looking around at everything, He left for Bethany with the twelve, since it was already late." (Mark 11:11). He entered Jerusalem, then left to walk to Bethany. That would be His pattern for the week—back and forth between the two cities. Each morning He and His disciples walked into Jerusalem for the day. At night, they returned to Bethany. During one of the daily transits, Jesus did something that at first glance seems totally uncharacteristic for Him. "On the next day, when they had left Bethany, He became hungry. Seeing at a distance a fig tree in leaf, He went to see if perhaps He would find anything on it; and when He came to it, He found nothing but leaves, for it was not the season for figs. He said to it, 'May no one ever eat fruit from you again!' And His disciples were listening." (Mark 11:12-14).

This story always bothered me. It seemed like Jesus was throwing a temper tantrum. He did not get the fruit He was expecting so He cursed the tree. Jesus seemed grouchy, ticked off. He needed a good cup of coffee or something. So He curses the tree, and of course, it dies because He is God. It all seemed so childish, so carnal. It made me uncomfortable. So it was one of those stories that I avoided. I was uncomfortable with that side of Jesus. What if I didn't do something He wanted? Would He curse me? Were His moods so fickle that He misbehaved like the capricious gods of Roman mythology?

But the fact that Jesus appeared to act like an adolescent wasn't the only awkward part of this story. Mark tells us that when He found no fruit on the tree, He spoke to the tree. That's a little strange, isn't it? If you saw your neighbor outside yelling at his tree, wouldn't you think that a little odd? That's the kind of thing someone would record and post to Facebook. And Jesus' "episode" didn't end with that. "Then they came to Jerusalem. And He entered the temple and began to drive out those who were buying and selling in the temple, and overturned the tables of the money changers and the seats of those who were selling doves." (Mark 11:15). It looks like Jesus is out of control. He doesn't get His breakfast, and now He's taking it out on the people in the Temple. I just didn't expect Jesus to be a hot head. But that's what He looks like. At least, that's how I used to think about this story. It was doctor Durham's devotional that helped me see things differently. Jesus did not behave poorly. He was not pitching a fit. Everything He did was intentional. This was not a childish reaction. As we dig deeper into this story, we will discover Jesus was making a well-calculated move. When we read the "rest of the story" as Paul Harvey used to say, a clearer picture begins to emerge. "When evening came, they would go out of the city. As they were passing by in the morning, they saw the fig tree withered from

> I was uncomfortable with that side of Jesus. What if I didn't do something He wanted? Would He curse me? Were His moods so fickle that He misbehaved like the capricious gods of Roman mythology?

the roots up. Being reminded, Peter said to Him, 'Rabbi, look, the fig tree which You cursed has withered.'" (Mark 11:19-21).

Picture this in your mind. The day before, Jesus cursed the tree, and then turned over the tables in the Temple. Now it's the next day and we are heading back into Jerusalem. We are walking on the same path we did yesterday. We pass by the spot where the tree was and Peter notices the tree is now dead. What do you think we would do? Would we give a passing glance, then keep walking? I don't think so. I know exactly what I would do. I would take a closer look. I think that's exactly what the disciples did. They gathered around that tree to check it out. And it's right there that this whole story starts to make sense. Jesus had an attentive audience. He had just set up one of the most incredible object lessons ever taught. The Master set up a teaching opportunity they would never forget—a teaching that has literally changed my life. I pray this teaching will impact your life as well.

1
A Lot Can Happen In 24 Hours

When the disciples stood around that tree to check it out, it had been 24 hours since Jesus cursed it. One of the first things Mark tells us is they noticed the tree had withered from the roots up. "As they were passing by in the morning, they saw the fig tree withered from the roots up." (Mark 11:20). That's not normal. Trees don't wither from the roots up. They wither from the branches down. That means this tree died backwards. Years ago I cut a tree down in my front yard. I left the stump, intending to get to it sometime in the future. The next spring there were shoots growing out of the stump. I drilled holes in the stump and poured poison into them. The following spring—more shoots. That thing wouldn't die. The trunk, branches and leaves were long gone—burned in my wood stove the winter before, but there was life under the ground. I finally had to have someone grind the stump and dig the roots out of the ground. Though I cut down the tree, there was still life under ground. That was not the case with the fig tree. When Jesus cursed the tree, death occurred in the roots, and then worked its way up into the branches. The tree died backwards.

> Trees don't wither from the roots up. They wither from the branches down. That means this tree died backwards.

I like the way Mark relays Jesus' response to the disciples. "And Jesus **answered** saying to them…" (Mark 11:22 emphasis added). The disciples had questions and Jesus was going to answer them. The first thing Jesus said to them was, "have faith in God." (Mark 11:22). That tells us the point of the lesson was to teach them about faith. This tree illustrates several lessons about faith. One of the first things it teaches is about the nature of the invisible realm. When did the tree die? I would suggest it died the moment Jesus cursed it. That was the day before, 24 hours earlier. The moment Jesus spoke to the tree, its life was snuffed from its roots. But the disciples didn't know that. From their perspective, nothing happened. That's because the tree died backwards. It wasn't until 24 hours later the disciples saw the results of what Jesus had done the day before. They could not see what was going on because the roots were invisible to them. Death had to work its way from the roots up into the branches.

Jesus created a picture of the relationship between the spiritual and the physical realm. As we will see, His teaching will make that abundantly clear. We live simultaneously in two realms—the physical and the spiritual. The spiritual realm is invisible, while the physical realm is perceived by our five senses. The roots of the tree were under ground, hidden from sight. They represent the spiritual realm. The branches represent the physical world. Though it may not be apparent, the two are connected.

> If something for God is going to happen in the physical realm, it must first be initiated in the spiritual.

Jesus demonstrated through this that what happens in the invisible realm, under the ground, away from sight, affects the physical realm. There is a cause-effect relationship between the two. If something for God is going to happen in the physical realm, it must first be initiated in the spiritual.

Our natural tendency is to measure reality by the things we can see, smell, taste, touch and hear. But the greater reality is in the invisible realm. The Apostle Paul said, "While we look not at the things which are seen, but at the things which are not seen; for the things which are seen are temporal, but the things which are not seen are eternal." (2 Corinthians 4:18). Everything in this physical world will not last. God measures reality by what remains. That invisible world is more real than this physical world. The realm of the roots is greater than the realm of the branches. Scripture makes it clear that it is always first the spiritual and then the physical. "By faith we understand that the worlds were prepared by the word of God, so that what is seen was not made out of things which are visible." (Hebrews

11:3). God, who is Spirit, spoke. Then the physical, material world came into being—first the spiritual—then the physical.

When instructing us to pray, Jesus demonstrated the relationship between the two. "Truly I say to you, whatever you bind on earth shall have been bound in heaven; and whatever you loose on earth shall have been loosed in heaven." (Matthew 18:18). According to Jesus' statement, whatever is bound on earth, has already been bound in heaven. Heaven leads the way and earth follows. Jesus taught us to pray, "Your kingdom come. Your will be done, on earth as it is in heaven." (Matthew 6:10). His will is established in heaven, then lived out on earth. Jesus used the fig tree to teach that principle. He wanted His disciples to understand that relationship because that cause-effect connection is vital for those who wish to live by faith.

And at the heart of this teaching, Jesus is talking about faith. When He "answers" their questions, He begins by saying, "Have faith in God." (Mark 11:22). This whole thing is about faith. I can picture Jesus casually responding to the disciple's amazement over the tree. "Have faith in God." The inference is, "What are you so amazed at? The tree died yesterday. The miracle was 24 hours ago. You are just now observing it, but the miracle happened yesterday. You need to have faith in God."

Jesus' response also reveals what should be the object of our faith. Our faith should be "in God". Our faith is only as reliable as its object. We must not place faith in our prayers, our church, or pastor, or even our own faith. It rests solely in God. When Jesus cursed the tree, they should have taken Him at His word. Of course, it is natural they did not understand right away. We probably would not have either. In retrospect, however, we can see that when Jesus commands something, it is done, whether we can physically see it or not.

What we need is already ours at the root. We have it in the spirit, but it must be manifested into our experience. And the key to that manifestation is faith. Faith is the bridge that moves things from the roots into the branches. Faith is vital to our spiritual lives. "And without faith it is impossible to please Him, for he who comes to God must believe that He is and that He is a rewarder of those who seek Him." (Hebrews 11:6). James said if we operate outside of faith, nothing will ever move from the roots into the branches. "But if any of you lacks wisdom, let him ask of God, who gives to all generously and without reproach, and it will be given to him. But he must ask in faith without any doubting, for the one who doubts is like the surf of the sea, driven and tossed by the wind. For that man ought not to expect that he will receive anything from the Lord, being a double-minded man, unstable in all his ways." (James 1:5-8). In fact, Jesus was hindered from fully expressing His power on one occasion because of the pervasive, corporate unbelief in His home territory. "And He did not do many miracles there because of their unbelief." (Matthew 13:58). Mark's gospel is even stronger, saying that His work was more than hindered, but stopped because of unbelief. "And He could do no miracle there except that He laid His hands on a few sick people and healed them." (Mark 6:5). Faith is vitally important. Jesus wanted His disciples to understand how it works.

Paul spoke of faith being a type of law. "Where then is boasting? It is excluded. By what kind of law? Of works? No, but by a law of faith." (Romans 3:27). The word "law" in this verse is with a small "L". So this is not speaking of Law, as in the commandments of God. But rather, this is referring to a principle within God's kingdom. There are "laws" or rules and ways faith operates. For example, we speak about the law of gravity. We are referring to the ways in which gravity operates. No matter how light you feel, if you step off a bridge, you are going to drop because of the law of gravity. That's simple. We get it. But there are also laws that relate to faith. Because of that, it's important we understand what faith is and what it isn't.

The writer to Hebrews gives us a starting place, though not an exhaustive definition. "Now faith is the assurance of things hoped for, the conviction of things not seen." (Hebrews 11:1). Hope is referring to the expectation for a better future. Faith is different than hope. It refers to seizing what one hopes for as a present reality. The word assurance refers to an inward confidence, and conviction is a determination to lay hold of something. Putting that together, it means faith lays hold of future expectations as a present reality. It believes it possesses now what it cannot see. It believes God has already accomplished His promise in the root—in the invisible, spiritual realm and waits in expectation for it to manifest in the branches. It moves God's answers from the roots into the branches.

That means that faith is far more than a belief. It is an action. Matthew shows what that looks like in the story of a woman who sought Jesus for healing. "And a woman who had been suffering from a hemorrhage for twelve years, came up behind Him and touched the fringe of His cloak; for she was saying to herself, 'If I only touch His garment, I will get well.' But Jesus turning and seeing her said, 'Daughter, take courage; your faith has made you well.' At once the woman was made well." (Matthew 9:20-22). Notice verse 21 specifically says she acted because she believed if she touched his garment she would get well. But in order to touch Jesus, she had to get through a sardine can of people who were pressing against Jesus. Because of her disease, she was

> Faith's action creates a bridge to bring the promises of God into our experience.

considered unclean and not allowed to mix with society. So she crawled through a forest of legs to get to Him. She did not just believe. She acted on her belief. Her belief was accurate. If she touched Him, she would be healed. That was a fact whether she touched Him or not. But if she hadn't fought her way through the crowd to get to Him, she would have never been healed. The knowledge alone wasn't enough. She had to act on her belief in order to experience what she believed. Faith's action creates a bridge to bring the promises of God into our experience. This is so important because Jesus ties it to mountains. "And Jesus answered saying to them, 'Have faith in God. Truly I say to you, whoever says to this mountain, "Be taken up and cast into the sea," and does not doubt in his heart, but believes that what he says is going to happen, it will be granted him."" (Mark 11:22-23).

We need a caveat, however. We need to act on our faith, but we also need to understand what faith is not. This is not about trying to make God do something for you. Jesus is not saying if you believe the roots are withered, He will go ahead and actually wither them for you. No. Faith believes the roots are already withered and because we believe that, it opens the door for them to manifest in the branches. Faith does not create its own reality. It is not some kind of magic power that causes things to happen. Faith is about accepting the reality God has already decreed. If I am trying to create reality by my faith, then that betrays the fact that I don't believe God has already done it. Therefore, my faith becomes more about me trying to overcome God's reluctance and convince Him to act on my behalf. That reverses the order to the two realms. It is always the spiritual realm first, and then the earthly realm follows.

It is important to understand that what we need, we already have. God has already granted us what we need. "…seeing that His divine power has granted to us everything pertaining to life and godliness, through the true knowledge of Him who called us by His own glory and excellence." (2 Peter 1:3). Everything we need for life and godliness is already granted, but it's waiting to manifest in our experience. Jesus touches on this in the way He shares the principle. "Therefore I say to you, all things for which you pray and ask believe that you have received them and they shall be granted you." (Mark 11:24). Jesus mixed a past tense and a present tense together, which on the surface doesn't make sense. Grammatically, He should have said, "Believe that **you shall receive** them and **they shall be granted** you." But that's not what He said. He said, "…believe that **you have received** them and **they shall be** granted to you." That means you currently don't have it, but you already do, and then you will.

Let's say I am going to pray to receive a red ball. Jesus' instruction means that I am not to ask God to give me a red ball and then He will. Instead, I am to believe that I already have the red ball (even though I don't) and then God will give it to me. Does that mean we are to pretend we have something we don't? That sounds like wishful thinking at best, but more likely a denial of reality. But don't forget, when Jesus said those words He was standing around that fig tree with His disciples. They were looking at a tree that died backwards. His words have to be understood in that context. Jesus is drawing a contrast between the roots and the branches. The roots died the day before when no one could see them. The branches were also as good as dead, but the effects of their death could not be seen until the next day. Remember, the roots represent the spiritual realm; the branches represent the physical realm. Jesus is saying that when we pray we are to believe we have already received what we ask for in the root—the spiritual realm, and then it will be granted in the branches— the physical realm. Faith declares it is done now, in the root. Faith doesn't say God will do it, but that God has already done it. Now we are just waiting for it to manifest in the physical realm.

This lesson has become very close to my heart because when I first learned this truth I determined to put it into practice. I have witnessed over and over again how the Lord has manifested something in the branches when I have clung by faith to the roots. I used to suffer regularly from severe migraines. I frequently experienced three different symptoms. I had a pounding headache that would drive me to bed. I had to be in a dark, cool room. It interrupted my life at the most inconvenient times. The second symptom was nausea. If not taken care of, the headache would progress until I became nauseous to the point of vomiting. The third symptom I can only describe as a lightning bolt that exploded in my head. This type of pain would strike for only a second or two. I was grateful for that because the pain was so severe that if it persisted any longer it would drop me to my knees.

I had sought healing for my migraines many times, but with no relief. At one point while I was praying over them (just when I was learning about the roots and branches) the Lord impressed me to pray and believe in the root for healing. I can distinctly remember the Saturday I prayed for healing. I was pastoring in Presque Isle, Maine at the time. We had a Saturday night service. Just before the service, I prayed alone in my office and then took my medication and dumped it in the toilet. That night I shared with my congregation what I had done and asked them to join me in praising God that it was accomplished in the root.

That Saturday night when I got home my head began to hurt. I decided to not ask God to take the pain away or to heal me. Instead, I believed He already had healed me in the root. So I gave Him praise. At two in the morning I was awakened with severe pain. I went down stairs and paced the floor, giving God praise—even though my head was pounding. I chose not to take any medication. I had dumped my prescription meds, but I chose to not even take an aspirin. I continued to pace and praise for two and a half hours. By 4:30 I was still in great pain and very aware that I had to preach the Sunday sermon in a few hours. At that time I said, "Lord, I am choosing to trust you, but I am getting weary and You know I have to preach. Please call someone to pray for me?" Two hours later (at 6:30) my headache disappeared. That is a miracle, because I had never once had a headache go away without heavy medication. Later that day I got a call from a man in our congregation who asked me if I was all right. He said the Lord had awakened him at 4:30 and he felt compelled to intercede for me until 6:00, when suddenly the burden was relieved. I praised God for I saw the answer beginning to manifest in the branches.

That afternoon a second wave of headaches came upon me. This time it was the kind that would drive me to nausea. I felt compelled to call one of my staff members, Doug Taubin. I wanted him to pray with me because I was so sick. When my wife, Marcia phoned him, he and his wife, Tina, were in their car close to where we lived. They came immediately over as well as another one of my prayer partners, Dr. Greg Blackstone. They gathered around my bed to pray for me. I remember tears were flowing down my cheek. I shared with them, however, that they were not tears of pain, but of joy because I saw a pattern. The first wave of headaches the night before was the one very distinct kind of headache I frequently suffered from. The Lord withered that branch early that morning. This was the other kind of headache I often experienced. I believed the Lord was going to manifest His answer in the branches concerning this type of headache as well. I told my friends not to pray I be healed, but to believe with me that it had been done in the root. We then thanked God it would manifest in the branches.

> We have no problem with the idea that God can do it. We are stretched a little more if we confess that God will do it. But that is not faith that moves mountains. We need to believe that God has already done it in the root and then wait for it to manifest in the branches.

I went to church that night and shared with the congregation what had happened thus far. I told them I was still suffering and therefore, going home. I asked them to pray for me by thanking God His answer had come and would manifest soon. They gladly did so. There was a group of men, led by Pastor Doug who decided to stay at church and pray until they felt released by God. I thank God for those men, because they prayed, literally on their faces, until midnight. At precisely that time, they felt released to stop and go home. It was that exact moment that the second wave of headaches stopped. That kind of headache has never come back. That has been over 15 years ago.

The next night I was watching a sermon on television. The pastor was talking about when one of his children was born. He said the family was gathered in the delivery room with him and his wife, but when the labor pains came and the birth was at hand, his wife ordered everyone out. He then related that to our spiritual journey and said there are times when the Lord calls us to be in delivery alone. At that moment the Lord spoke to my spirit and said the last wave of headaches was something I had to face alone.

Sure enough, that night the "lightning bolt" headaches struck me late in the evening after everyone had gone to bed. I was awakened from sleep by the pain. I quietly slipped out of bed and went to the kitchen. As I had said, this type of headache would only strike for a second or two. There would never be more than one or two spasms of pain. That night the lightening was flashing continually. I knew, however, from what the Lord had said earlier that I had to be in the delivery room alone. I paced the kitchen, praising God that He was manifesting His answer in the branches. After thirty minutes, the pain abruptly stopped. It has never come back, Praise the Lord!

I have prayed according to this principle for the last 25 years. I have often wondered why there is almost always a delay between the answer in the roots and its manifestation in the branches. When Jesus cursed the fig tree the delay was intentional. He could have caused the entire tree to immediately shrivel up before the disciples' eyes. But instead, He caused the delay as part of His object lesson on faith. I believe the delay is God's system for building our faith. If the branches withered instantly every time we prayed there would be no need for faith. The delay teaches us to trust His Word, even when circumstances say otherwise. This will take an adjustment in our thinking. We have no problem with the idea that God can do it. We are stretched a little more if we confess that God will do it. But that is not faith that moves mountains. We need to believe that God has already done it in the root and then wait for it to manifest in the branches. I understand it's not logical to declare I have something when it's obvious I don't, but that's how faith works. We're not dealing with our senses; we are dealing with faith. We are dealing with the spiritual realm and bringing its fruit into manifestation. So is this as simple as believing we already have what we ask for? Yes, and no. Believing at the root is the starting point, but Jesus had a lot more to teach His disciples while they stood around that tree. My hope is that as we drill down into the meaning of His words, our understanding will expand, our faith will grow and our lives will be changed.

2
Don't Think Mustard Seeds—Think Trees

"Jesus entered Jerusalem and came into the temple; and after looking around at everything, He left for Bethany with the twelve, since it was already late. On the next day, when they had left Bethany, He became hungry. Seeing at a distance a fig tree in leaf, He went to see if perhaps He would find anything on it; and when He came to it, He found nothing but leaves, for it was not the season for figs. He said to it, 'May no one ever eat fruit from you again!' And His disciples were listening." (Mark 11:11-14).

When evening came, they would go out of the city. As they were passing by in the morning, they saw the fig tree withered from the roots up. Being reminded, Peter said to Him, 'Rabbi, look, the fig tree which You cursed has withered.' And Jesus answered saying to them, 'Have faith in God.'" (Mark 11:19-22).

If we could reduce Jesus' teaching down to two words, they would be, "Have faith." (Mark 9:22). Everything else will supplement that idea. It is a command. We must have faith. But how do we do that? We either believe or we don't. How can we have faith if we don't? How do we believe that we believe when we actually don't believe? If we don't have faith, we can't create it. But here is the wonderful truth—If we are followers of Christ, we do have faith already. Faith is a gift God gives every one of His children. The Apostle Paul said, "…by grace you have been saved through faith; and that not of yourselves, it is the gift of God." (Ephesians 2:8). We can only be saved if we have faith, but God gives us the necessary faith as a gift. Remember we already have everything we need for life and godliness (2 Peter 1:3). Paul opened his letter to the Ephesian church with that great truth. "Blessed be the God and Father of our Lord Jesus Christ, who has blessed us with every spiritual blessing in the heavenly places in Christ." (Ephesians 1:3). Whatever spiritual blessings we need, we already have them in Christ; including faith. Paul repeats this idea in his letter to the Romans. "For through the grace given to me I say to everyone among you not to think more highly of himself than he ought to think; but to think so as to have sound judgment, as **God has allotted to each a measure of faith**." (Romans 12:3 emphasis added).

That's good news. But if it's true, why do some people see God's promises manifest in the branches and others do not? That's because even though we are all given a measure of faith, it has to grow. Jesus spoke often of varying degrees of faith in different people. He rebuked His disciples because they were slow to believe. They watched Jesus feed 5000 men, plus women and children with a few loaves of bread and a couple fish. Shortly afterward, He did the same with 4000 men, plus women and children. The disciples saw Jesus provide for thousands of people from virtually nothing. It was such a great miracle; it was recorded in all four gospels. Not long after that, Jesus and His disciples were getting into a boat to sail across the Sea of Galilee. He told them to beware of the leaven of the Pharisees. They didn't get what He meant and thought perhaps He was warning them because they hadn't remembered to bring some bread with them for their journey. Jesus overheard them talking about it. They had just watched him provide bread for so many; surely He could provide a meal while on the boat if needed. Matthew says, "But Jesus, aware of this, said, 'You men of **little faith**, why do you discuss among yourselves that you have no bread?'" (Matthews 16:8 emphasis added). They had faith, but it was little faith.

On another occasion Jesus was asked to heal a Gentile ruler's dying servant. Jesus was ready to head to the man's home, but the man stopped Him. He didn't feel worthy to have Jesus come under his roof. He told Jesus he understood how authority works, because he commands men and they do his bidding. So he told Jesus he was confident if Jesus just said the word, his servant would be healed, even though Jesus did not go to his home. Jesus was amazed at the amount of faith in this Gentile ruler. Matthew says, "Now when Jesus heard this, He marveled and said to those who were following, 'Truly I say to you, I have not found such **great faith** with anyone in Israel.'" (Matthew 8:10 emphasis added). The man's faith was great. The disciples' faith was little. Some have little faith and some have great faith, but they all have a measure of faith. That's good news, but it almost seems unfair. Why was I only given a little faith when someone else was given great faith? That's actually the wrong question.

The Apostle Peter teaches us that God treats us all alike. "God is not one to show partiality." (Acts 10:34). God doesn't give one great faith while only giving another a little bit of faith. Each is given a measure, but it's up to us to develop our faith. Faith is like a muscle; it can grow, or it can shrink. Paul speaks of a growing faith in 2 Corinthians. "…not boasting beyond our measure, that is, in other men's labors, but with the hope that **as your faith grows**, we will be, within our sphere, enlarged even more by you." (2 Corinthians 10:15 emphasis added). But then he also mentions the possibility of one's faith becoming weak. Abraham was promised he and his wife, Sarah, would have a child in their old age. That was impossible and Abraham was well aware of his and his wife's inability to produce a child. That's where Paul says, "Without **becoming weak in faith** he contemplated his own body, now as good as dead since he was about a hundred years old, and the deadness of Sarah's womb; yet, with respect to the promise of God, he did not waver in unbelief but grew strong in faith, giving glory to God." (Romans 4:19-20 emphasis added). His faith never weakened, but the way Paul writes, it appears it could have. Like a muscle our faith can grow strong, or it can atrophy.

If Abraham had paid attention to what his senses perceived, his faith would have weakened. He was too old to have a child. She was too old. There were no purple pills back then! Enough said. But instead of dwelling on his impotence, he focused on the word of God. He paid attention to God's promise and his faith strengthened. But watch this—it's not that he denied his old age. He didn't engage in some New Age mantra, and stand in front of a mirror and repeat ten times a day that he was young and his age was just an illusion. He was realistic about the impossibility of his situation. Age was a fact. He couldn't deny that, but—this is vital—he chose not to pay attention to it. He chose to ignore the facts and focus on the promises of God. Yes, he was old, but God's word promised him an heir. Both were realities and both were in conflict. But Abraham chose to focus on the facts of God's word, rather than the facts of his physical condition.

Every one of us can do this. In fact I'm guessing many of you already have at one time or another. Let me explain. Many of you may recall a time when you were in a hurry and had to stop into a store to pick something up before heading to another obligation. You were rushing through the aisles to get the things you needed, when you turned the corner and noticed at the end of the aisle *that* person. You know—the one who if they saw you would start talking without taking a breath, and keep you there for 20 minutes. You like them, but you just don't have the time to talk, and you don't want to be rude. So what do you do? If you've been in that situation, I know what you did, because I have done it too. You pretended you didn't see them, and you quickly slipped into the next aisle before they saw you. You were aware of their presence, but you ignored them. Don't judge me—you know you've done it, just like I have. That's how Abraham's faith grew. He ignored the circumstances of his aged body, and instead concentrated on the promises of God.

> Abraham chose to focus on the facts of God's word, rather than the facts of his physical condition.

The disciples recognized the need for their faith to grow. They pleaded with Jesus, "Increase our faith!" (Luke 17:5). To increase means to expand that which already exists. They didn't need God to give them more faith. They had already been given a measure of faith from God. But they did need the faith they already possessed to grow. They needed to exercise that muscle and watch it expand.

The other day someone left a bike at church. I had the bright idea that I would take it home and ride it to work the next day. It is only a two-mile trip. When I was a kid I rode my bike all over town. This would be fun, even though I hadn't ridden a bike in 30 years. Five minutes into the trip I knew it was a mistake. How could this have ever been fun? By the time I arrived at church my thighs were shaking and I was such a mass of sweat I had to go back home and take another shower. I hadn't exercised those muscles in years. I learned you can't jump on a bike and start riding. You have to build up to it. That's how we often treat our faith. We don't exercise it regularly and then when there's an emergency we try to jump on the bike and believe God for a miracle. If we don't develop the muscle, we may find our faith too weak to move a mountain.

But doesn't the Bible say all we need to move a mountain is the faith of a mustard seed? That's the smallest of seeds. Jesus said, "truly I say to you, if you have faith the size of a mustard seed, you will say to this mountain, 'Move from here to there,' and it will move; and nothing will be impossible to you.'" (Matthew 17:20). If my faith is the size of a mustard seed (the size of a small muscle) isn't that enough? It sure sounds like that is what Jesus is teaching. But if we read Jesus' entire statement we see what looks like a

> The characteristic of the mustard seed Jesus was emphasizing was not that it was tiny, but that even though it started out small, it had the potential to grow into a tree large enough for the birds to nest in it.

contradiction. "And He said to them, 'Because of the littleness of your faith; for truly I say to you, if you have faith the size of a mustard seed, you will say to this mountain, "Move from here to there," and it will move; and nothing will be impossible to you.'" (Matthew 17:20).

The disciples had tried to cast a demon out of a boy, but were unsuccessful. They were exasperated, because nothing they tried worked. Finally, Jesus arrived on scene and in a few minutes the demon was eradicated and the boy was healed. The disciples were confused, because just a few days earlier they had been sent out to the surrounding villages to preach the good news. On many occasions they cast out demons. That's why they were confident they could cast the demon out of this boy, and were shocked when they couldn't. After the incident, they privately asked Jesus why they couldn't do it. He told them it was because of the littleness of their faith (Matthew 17:20). Their faith was too small to cast that particular demon out. But then Jesus said if their faith was the size of a mustard seed, nothing would be impossible to them. Do you see the contradiction? All they needed to cast out the demon was a little faith. But that's what they had, and that's the reason they couldn't cast it out. It's as if Jesus said, "The reason you couldn't do what you tried to do is because your faith is too little. What's the answer? You need little faith. Then you could do what you tried to do."

That doesn't make any sense. They couldn't do it because their faith was too little. But all they needed to do it was little faith. That's like saying the price to get into the show is one dollar. But when you hand the teller a dollar they refuse you admittance because a dollar isn't enough to get in. It's a logical contradiction. That's why I think Jesus was driving at something else. The characteristic of the mustard seed Jesus was emphasizing was not that it was tiny, but that even though it started out small, it had the potential to grow into a tree large enough for the birds to nest in it. The mustard seed starts small but grows very large. In the same way, our faith starts small but must be developed.

When the Apostle Paul wanted to drive home the importance of faith for salvation, he spotlighted the patriarch, Abraham.

What then shall we say that Abraham, our forefather according to the flesh, has found? For if Abraham was justified by works, he has something to boast about, but not before God. For what does the Scripture say? "Abraham believed God, and it was credited to him as righteousness." (Romans 4:1-3).

For this reason it is by faith, in order that it may be in accordance with grace, so that the promise will be guaranteed to all the descendants, not only to those who are of the Law, but also to those who are of the faith of Abraham, who is the father of us all. (Romans 4:16).

Without becoming weak in faith he contemplated his own body, now as good as dead since he was about a hundred years old, and the deadness of Sarah's womb; yet, with respect to the promise of God, he did not waver in unbelief but grew strong in faith, giving glory to God, and being fully assured that what God had promised, He was able also to perform. Therefore it was also credited to him as righteousness. (Romans 4:19-22).

Verse 20 says that Abraham grew strong in faith, but he didn't start there. He had many stumbles along the way as his faith developed. When God first called Abraham, He told him to leave his father and mother and move away. Abraham did pack his bags and go, but he didn't obey fully. He took his father and nephew, Lot, with him. He had faith enough to leave, but his faith was still small. He wouldn't separate from his father until his father died. Even then, when moving on, after his father's death, he took Lot with him. Over and over God ran Abraham through many tests to strengthen his faith. Sometimes Abraham succeeded, but many times he failed.

When there was a famine in the land, instead of trusting God, he moved to Egypt where there was plenty of food. That was a fail. And while there he threw his wife, Sarai, under the bus, telling the Pharaoh she was his sister so they wouldn't kill Abraham and take his wife. Sarai was beautiful, and Pharaoh did take her into his harem, but spared Abraham's life. God rescued Sarai from being violated by

Pharaoh. Those were trials that tested Abraham's faith. Even though he failed, God looked out for him, and in the process strengthened Abraham to believe God was his protector. This fear of losing his life due to his wife's beauty was apparently a weak spot with Abraham, because he faced the same situation again with King Abimelech. And again he passed Sarai off as his sister in order to save his own neck. Those were all tests to build his faith, and Abraham failed them. But God used even his failures to strengthen his faith.

There were other times when he passed the tests. When the land was getting too small to feed both his and Lot's flocks, they had to go their separate ways. This was the moment when Abraham finally left his old family as God had originally commanded him. When it came to it, Abraham passed the faith test. He looked out over the land with his nephew and offered Lot the first choice of land. If Lot chose the north, he would go south, and visa versa. Abraham was the patriarch of the family. By rights he could have chosen the land first and given Lot the leftovers. But he trusted God and allowed Lot to choose. The direction toward Sodom was lush and green. The other direction was barren and dry. Lot chose the fruitful land, so Abraham moved into the desert. He trusted God to care for him. That was a faith win.

The New Testament points out the great faith Abraham had to believe God would give him and Sarah (no longer Sarai at this point) a son. But he didn't believe that way at first. His faith had to grow. Thirteen years earlier, he slept with Sarah's maiden, Hagar, to produce a son. Ishmael was born to Abraham and Hagar. Sarah had reasoned that perhaps God wanted to fulfill His promise through Abraham, but not necessarily through her. So she proposed Abraham have a child through Hagar. Abraham eventually believed, but not at first. It took time and tests for his faith to grow. The ultimate test was when God commanded Abraham to take Isaac, the promised child, and sacrifice him on an altar.

Isaac represented everything Abraham and Sarah had lived for. All their hopes were wrapped up in that child. The entire purpose they originally left home was to produce a family that would become the ancestors of the promised Messiah, the savior of the world. Everything depended on the child Isaac. But God called Abraham to lay all of that down. It was the greatest faith test of his life. Abraham passed the test. "By faith Abraham, when he was tested, offered up Isaac, and he who had received the promises was offering up his only begotten son; it was he to whom it was said, 'In Isaac your descendants shall be called.' He considered that God is able to raise people even from the dead, from which he also received him back as a type." (Hebrews 11:17-19). If Abraham already had a child when God called him to leave his home and family, and if God had commanded he sacrifice his child at the beginning of his faith journey, Abraham probably would not have done it. When he agreed to sacrifice Isaac, he had great faith, but it did not start that way. His faith developed over time and trials. Ours must grow as well. There will be victories and failures. We will stumble, mess up, fall back a few steps, but there will also be many wins along the way. It is all part of God's plan to develop that mustard seed of faith into a great tree.

God also gave many encouragements along the way. On more than one occasion God told Abraham to look at the night sky and promised him his family would be as many as the stars above. He also cut a covenant with Abraham, promising him a great family. He eventually changed Abraham's name. Originally it was Abram. But God changed it to Abraham, which means father of many nations. He also changed Sarah's name. Originally it was Sarai, which meant quarrelsome. Sarah meant princess, indicating she and her husband would be rulers over many.

Many of Abraham's tests had no logical purpose other than faith development. Why leave home? Why become a nomad? Why offer your child on an altar? Many of God's promptings served no logical purpose. They were simply designed to develop Abraham's faith. I have watched this happen many times. God has called people to do things that have no apparent purpose. What they do does not even seem logical. But often His callings serve a purpose we can't at first see. Sometimes it is simply to exercise our muscle.

I was sitting in the congregation during the singing time in our worship service. Suddenly, without any fanfare, a man about four rows ahead of me, stepped out into the aisle, got down on all fours and started doing pushups! He pumped off about ten, then got up and returned to his seat. Weird. The service went on as if nothing had happened. Later we asked him about it. He said he sensed the Holy Spirit prompting him to do that. He hesitated at first, knowing it would be awkward, but he was seeking to hear the Lord's voice and obey His subtle nudges. As far as he knew, that's all there was to the story. Perhaps God was testing him to see how willing he was to obey. We learned later there was more to the story than any of us could have known. A woman was visiting church that Saturday night. She was wrestling with God, wondering if He was real. In desperation she lifted up a private prayer while the congregation was singing. "God, if you are real, then make someone do something unusual. Um, make someone get down and do some pushups." When she saw the young man do exactly that, she was thunderstruck. She didn't really expect anything to happen. But when it did, she could not deny the reality of God. That very night she gave her life to Jesus.

I remember when I first made a conscious attempt to respond to faith challenges from the Lord. Our small church in Maine was struggling along. We were a traditional church with a little over 100 people, most of them senior citizens. I was walking in my prayer closet (a local park) meditating and praying about the church. There was a passage in Isaiah 43 that caught my attention.

Do not fear, for I am with you; I will bring your offspring from the east, and gather you from the west. I will say to the north, "Give them up!" And to the south, "Do not hold them back."

Bring My sons from afar and My daughters from the ends of
the earth, everyone who is called by My name, and whom I
have created for My glory, whom I have formed, even whom I
have made. Bring out the people who are blind, even though
they have eyes, and the deaf, even though they have ears.
(Isaiah 43:5-8).

Isaiah spoke of those who have eyes but are blind, and who are
deaf, though they have ears. This is speaking about the spiritually
blind and deaf. That tugged at my heart and I began to pray for the lost
in our area. I knew the context of this passage was about scattered
Israel being brought back into the land, but I kept thinking of those in
Aroostook County, Maine. As I walked and prayed, I kept thinking
about the north, south, east and west. Suddenly a thought came to me.
As I investigated it, I sensed God was prompting me to do something.
It was a little odd but I felt the Lord was directing me. I was seeking to
live in obedience and trying to learn how to trust God's promptings.
So I decided to go for it. I called my prayer partner, Phil, and told him
I wanted to take him somewhere. We arrived at Mantle Lake Park and
got out of my truck. I told him we needed to take a hike through the
woods. Off I went, with Phil following behind. The trail wound
through the woods, then across a potato field and finally to the top of a
hill. The hill was probably the highest point in our community. I read
the Scripture passage to Phil, then told him I sensed God wanted us to
face each direction of the compass and demand the enemy give up all
those who had eyes but could not see and ears, but could not hear. We
prayed with the authority of Christ as we faced each direction of the
compass. Once finished, we hiked back out. That was a little outside
our normal practice, but if nothing else, we had a nice hike. That
following Sunday we had 50 new guests in church—quite an increase
for a church running a little over 100. The amazing thing is, those
people never left. They became a part of our church. At that point

people started getting saved. We eventually grew to almost 800 people; a great number of them were converts to the faith.

A year or two later I was praying and had the same sense as before. This time I took the men's prayer group to the top of the hill. There were 40 of us. It was dark out, so we got in our pickups and all drove to the top. Locals must have wondered what was happening when 40 men drove trucks to the top of the hill. Again we prayed in the four directions of the compass. Once done, we drove home. That weekend, we jumped 100 people in attendance. I've told people over the years that kind of thing only works in response to the prompting of the Holy Spirit. Otherwise, I would have gone up there and prayed that way every week!

God was teaching us to trust His leadings. Our faith was growing as we stepped out in obedience to the direction of the Lord. God uses those kinds of things to grow our faith. When we stumble in a faith test, He can use that to reinforce His care for us when He walks along beside us to help us through the failure. When we are successful in the faith test, we will watch our faith muscles grow. The mustard seed can become a great tree. Sometimes I feel like mine is barely a sapling, but I know God is at work, guiding the growth of my faith. He will do the same with you as well, for Hebrews reminds us that Jesus is the author and finisher of our faith (Hebrews 12:2).

3
Speaking To Trees Is Like Talking To Mountains

"Being reminded, Peter said to Him, 'Rabbi, look, the fig tree which You cursed has withered.' And Jesus answered saying to them, 'Have faith in God. Truly I say to you, whoever says to this mountain, "Be taken up and cast into the sea," and does not doubt in his heart, but believes that what he says is going to happen, it will be granted him.'" (Mark 11:21-23). You might have noticed that Peter asked about the tree and Jesus responded by talking about a mountain. Did He shift their attention from the tree to some nearby mountain? Did Jesus abruptly change illustrations? I do not believe so. The New Testament was written in Greek, but Jesus spoke in Aramaic. The word for mountain in Aramaic means problem. We use the cliché, "making a mountain out of a molehill." Which means turning something small into a huge problem. So the concept of mountains representing problems is not unfamiliar. When Jesus taught His disciples, using the tree as an object lesson, He was talking about dealing with problems. In fact, in another passage, Jesus spoke about casting things into the sea, only in this one He used the metaphor of a tree. "And the Lord said, 'If you had faith like a mustard seed, you would say to this mulberry tree, "Be uprooted and be planted in the sea"; and it would obey you.'" (Luke 17:6). What Jesus meant was, "Whoever says to this problem be taken up and cast into the sea..."

The tree represented a problem and Jesus spoke directly to it. He taught His disciples and us that we have to speak directly to our problems. That sounds strange, kind of like talking to a tree. But that's what Jesus did, and that's what He is teaching us to do. If you are like me, when I pray about a problem, I am much more comfortable talking to God about my problem than I am talking directly to the problem. In fact, what I am hoping is that I can talk to God about my problem and then He will deal with it for me. But that's not what Jesus said to do. Jesus said we have to speak to our problem (mountain) and command it to be moved. We might wonder if Jesus literally meant that. It seems so silly to talk to the problem, but Jesus didn't just teach this principle,

He lived it. Jesus visited Peter's home and found Peter's mother-in-law was sick. Jesus healed her, but notice how Peter described it. "Then He got up and left the synagogue, and entered Simon's home. Now Simon's mother-in-law was suffering from a high fever, and they asked Him to help her. And standing over her, He rebuked the fever, and it left her; and she immediately got up and waited on them." (Luke 4:38-39). Jesus spoke to the fever. He didn't ask the Father to heal Peter's mother-in-law. He rebuked the fever directly. He spoke to the mountain...or the problem...or the tree. Why did Jesus instruct us to face our problems this way?

> Speaking to the mountain activates our faith. To believe God will deal with our mountain is good, but we have to act on that belief.

1. Speaking to the mountain activates our faith. To believe God will deal with our mountain is good, but we have to act on that belief. Otherwise, faith is only theoretical. Luke shows how acting on one's belief demonstrates that faith is real.

> And a woman who had a hemorrhage for twelve years, and could not be healed by anyone, came up behind Him and touched the fringe of His cloak, and immediately her hemorrhage stopped. And Jesus said, "Who is the one who touched Me?" And while they were all denying it, Peter said, "Master, the people are crowding and pressing in on You." But Jesus said, "Someone did touch Me, for I was aware that power had gone out of Me." When the woman saw that she had not escaped notice, she came trembling and fell down before Him, and declared in the presence of all the people the reason why she had touched Him, and how she had been immediately healed. And He said to her, "Daughter, your faith has made you well; go in peace." (Luke 8:43-48).

Jesus acted like He did not know who touched Him. Either He did that to draw attention to the woman, or He really did not know. Whichever it was, it is clear Jesus did not initiate the healing. The woman's actions released the healing power of Jesus. In verse 46 Jesus said, "Someone did touch Me, for I was aware that power had gone out of Me." That indicates that Jesus did not activate the power, but someone else did. When He turned to the woman He said to her, "Daughter, your faith has made you well." (Luke 8:48). This does not mean the woman healed herself. The power came from God. He is the one who healed her. If Jesus had not been willing, she couldn't have released the power from Him. He is not a spigot we can go to and simply turn on the power. He has to be willing, but honors faith that takes initiative.

When Jesus stood with His disciples around that tree, He told them to take action. He said, "Whoever says to this mountain…" (Mark 11:23). Speaking to the tree is a verbal action. He did not say if we believe the mountain will move, then it will move. He said we had to speak to the mountain and then it would be done. Saying what we believe is far more important than we may realize. In 2 Corinthians the Apostle Paul was talking about the many persecutions and hardships he endured because of the gospel. But then he quoted an Old Testament passage in order to make clear that because he believed the gospel, he had to declare it. "But having the same spirit of faith, according to what is written, 'I believed, therefore I spoke,' we also believe, therefore we also speak." (2 Corinthians 4:13). The spirit of faith is characterized by someone who believes and speaks out what he or she believes.

In another place, Paul wrote, "But what does it say? 'The word is near you, in your mouth and in your heart'—that is, the word of faith which we are preaching." (Romans 10:8). The word of faith Paul was talking about is the Scripture. He was saying that word is in our mouths. Why is the word of God in our mouths? It is there to speak it. Let's imagine we have been seeking the Lord for reassurance over a specific situation, and He impresses a promise on our hearts, confirming it as a word for us in that moment. Perhaps it is Philippians 4:19, "And my God will supply all your needs according to His riches in glory in Christ Jesus." We claim that verse and believe God will meet our need. But then circumstances look like the need isn't going to be met. What do we do? Do we complain that God is not going to keep His word? No. Do we go back to prayer and beg God all over again to meet our need? No. Instead, we stand in faith and confess the word of God. We might pray something like, "Lord I know the circumstances look bad, but I am not going to be influenced by them. I praise you and thank you that your word says you shall supply all my needs."

This is the way we build our faith muscle. Some people can run ten miles at a time, but they didn't start that way. When in college I ran six miles a day, and on weekends, I ran ten. But when I started running, it was more of a jog, interspersed with a lot of walking. Today it would have to be jogging interspersed with trips to the ER! I started slow and worked toward that goal. The confession of our faith is like walking. It is the beginning of the exercising of our faith. We begin there. Paul told Timothy to discipline himself for the purpose of godliness (1 Timothy 4:7). Holding fast the confession of our faith is the beginning of that discipline.

2. Jesus instructed us to speak to our mountain because God won't do what He has commanded us to do. It is our responsibility to speak to the mountains in our life. God has delegated authority to us and He expects us to use it. "And [so that you can know and understand] what is the immeasurable and unlimited and surpassing greatness of His power in and for us who believe, as demonstrated in the working of His mighty strength, which He exerted in Christ when He raised Him from the dead and seated Him at His [own] right hand in the heavenly [places]." (Eph.1:19-20, Amplified Bible). This is saying God's immeasurable power is working in us who believe; the same power that raised Jesus from the dead. That same power has authority over the enemy. Paul goes on to say that power is "far above

all rule and authority and power and dominion, and every name that is named, not only in this age but also in the one to come." (Ephesians 1:21). Because that power is in us, He has delegated it to us to use in His name.

James says, "Resist the devil and he will flee from you." (James 4:7b). To resist means to actively fight against. James is telling us it is our responsibility to actively fight against the devil. That means when Satan spiritually attacks us, we can't run to God and ask Him to fight the devil for us. We have to take the authority He has already delegated to us and use it. Jesus already defeated Satan. "The Son of God appeared for this purpose, to destroy the works of the devil." (1 John 3:8b). Jesus defeated Satan through His death and resurrection. And now He has delegated His authority to us (Matthew 28:18-20).

> When Satan spiritually attacks us, we can't run to God and ask Him to fight the devil for us. We have to take the authority He has already delegated to us and use it.

We may wonder why we have to fight Satan at all if he is already defeated. The Lord has allowed him limited authority on the earth. He no longer has the power of death, but he does use temptation, fear and deception to hinder God's children. We can't know for sure why God hasn't completely removed him, but we can understand part of the reason.

When Israel invaded the Promised Land of Canaan, they were instructed to dispossess all the inhabitants living there. They partially obeyed, but several tribes were left there—people who would prove to cause Israel much grief. The writer of the book of Judges tells us part of the reason. "Now these are the nations which the Lord left, to test Israel by them (that is, all who had not experienced any of the wars of Canaan; only in order that the generations of the sons of Israel

might be taught war, those who had not experienced it formerly)."
(Judges 3:1-2).

God allowed those nations to remain. We don't know all the reasons, but they were useful in teaching the next generation warfare. They needed to learn how to fight. That sounds brutal, but they lived in a different world than the one in which we live. The world will be much better when Satan is completely gone. And why he is not yet removed, I can't fully say. But, the advantage we can glean from his presence in this world is that we can learn how to fight. Paul called the walk of faith the "good fight" (1 Timothy 1:18, 6:12; 2 Timothy 4:7). We walk in this world by faith and we battle the forces of darkness by faith. His presence trains us to fight the good fight of faith. One of the reasons Satan still works so much destruction in the church is because believers haven't learned how to engage in the fight of faith. God has given us full authority. "Behold, I have given you authority to tread on serpents and scorpions, and over all the power of the enemy, and nothing will injure you." (Luke 10:19). So many times I have heard believers say the devil is attacking them and then ask me to pray that God will get the devil off their back. When they do I tell them no. "God has already given you full authority to resist the devil. Submit to God and resist the devil and he will flee from you. God is not going to resist him. You have to do that."

When I first moved to Maine to pastor a church in Presque Isle, we lived in a parsonage. Those are almost a thing of the past these days. But back then the church would often provide a house for the pastor. One night I was awakened and sat up in bed. I turned to the door that was immediately to my right. We kept it open in order to hear our two infant children. Our son was six months old and our daughter was 19 months old. When I looked down the hall outside our bedroom door, I saw a tall figure standing there. It looked like a man about six feet in height. I couldn't make out any features. He was in silhouette. I knew immediately it wasn't human.

Years earlier in my life, I had a season when I was harassed by demonic spirits. I lived in terror and would beg God to make it go away. Nothing seemed to help. But when this spirit appeared in my hallway, I was older and had been taught a little about spiritual warfare. I also had a family and perhaps that is what triggered something different in me. Instead of feeling fear, I felt rage. An anger rose up in me that rejected this intruder. With a hardened edge in my voice I spoke aloud, directly to the being. I said, "You have no authority to be in the home. In the name of Jesus Christ, I command you to leave." Immediately it disappeared. About a month later it happened again. This time I commanded the same thing, only I added, "I command you to leave and don't ever return." It left and never has returned.

We have authority in Christ. When we face a mountain He expects us to use the authority He has given us. If we submit our lives to God and then resist the devil, James promises us, he will flee from us. Jesus constantly taught this lesson to His disciples. On one occasion the disciples and Jesus were sailing across the Sea of Galilee when a great storm whipped up on the lake. Jesus was asleep in the bow, exhausted from extended hours of ministry. The disciples were seasoned fishermen, but they thought they were going to drown. They awakened Jesus to help them. Luke tells us, "They came to Jesus and woke Him up, saying, 'Master, Master, we are perishing!' And He got up and rebuked the wind and the surging waves, and they stopped, and it became calm. And He said to them, 'Where is your faith?' They were fearful and amazed, saying to one another, 'Who then is this, that He commands even the winds and the water, and they obey Him?'" (Luke 8:24-25). Notice Jesus didn't pray and ask God to calm the sea. Instead, He spoke directly to the storm. He commanded the mountain to be removed. When the disciples wondered at what He did, just like the fig tree, He spoke of faith.

The disciples eventually got it. Peter and John were walking to the temple to pray when a beggar, seeking alms, confronted them. "But

Peter, along with John, fixed his gaze on him and said, 'Look at us!' And he began to give them his attention, expecting to receive something from them. But Peter said, 'I do not possess silver and gold, but what I do have I give to you: In the name of Jesus Christ the Nazarene—walk!' And seizing him by the right hand, he raised him up; and immediately his feet and his ankles were strengthened." (Acts 3:4-6). Notice Peter and John never prayed for the man. They didn't ask God to heal him. Peter said, "What I have I give you." What did he have? The authority of Christ. He commanded the man, in the name of Jesus, to be healed. God commands us to take authority in His name and speak to our mountain. He won't do for us what He has commanded us to do.

3. Jesus instructed us to speak to our mountain because if we do not talk to our mountain, our mountain will talk to us. Satan's weapon is deception. His minions are constantly at work trying to whisper lies into our ears. He will bombard us with thoughts about why our problem is too big. Nehemiah was commissioned by God to lead an effort to rebuild the wall around Jerusalem. Israel had been in captivity for 70 years. The city of Jerusalem lay in ruins. Those living in the area were not pleased with Nehemiah's ambitions.

The resistance was led by a man named Sanballat. He is a type of Satan. His name means "hatred in disguise".[1] Lucifer is identified in the Bible as one who masquerades as an angel of light (2 Corinthians 11:4). Sanballat presents himself as a friend of the Jews, but in reality hates what they are doing. Nehemiah 4:1 says he "mocked the Jews". That word means "to scorn in order to demoralize".[2] It was a verbal attack he initiated against the Jews. Satan wages war in the same way. His method is effective because we often do not recognize the attack as the work of the enemy.

One reason is that the battle is waged in the mind. Satan cannot read our minds, but I believe he can plant thoughts there. When King Nebuchadnezzar had a disturbing dream, he called his wise men to interpret it. He knew they sometimes told him what he wanted to hear.

He was not interested in their maneuverings. He needed answers. What did the dream mean? To ensure they got their insight from the gods, he refused to tell them the dream. He wanted them to tell him the dream and its interpretation. If they could not do it, they would die.

Two groups were highly motivated in that scenario. The wise men wanted the answer in order to spare their lives. Satan and his angels wanted the answer so the wise men could continue to have the King's ear, and thus the demons could direct him through their human puppets. But no matter how they tried, the Magi could not reveal the dream, let alone its interpretation. That is because Satan could not read the King's mind. Only Daniel was able to reveal the dream, because God revealed it to him. (Daniel 2:1-49). Satan cannot read our minds. He does not have that omniscient power. However, he can plant thoughts into our minds.

> Like the Jews who were in captivity because of their sin, [Satan] reminds us of our failures.

We do not recognize his thoughts because they are disguised. He speaks to us in first person, singular. In other words, he would not whisper into our ears, "You are stupid." That would be too obvious. Instead, he whispers, "I am stupid". It sounds and feels like our own thinking. Sometimes it is, but often the enemy is there, feeding our minds with destructive thoughts with full immunity because he is disguised as us. Sanballat functioned in the Nehemiah story in the same way. He accused the Jews and in doing so revealed the way Satan tries to accuse us. This story reveals six ways Satan attacks us.

1. He attacks our identity. Sanballat said to any who would listen, "…what are these feeble Jews doing…" (Nehemiah 4:2). It is as if Sanballat was asking, "Who do you think you are? You are nothing but a feeble bunch of Jews. You are a defeated people. You have been in captivity for 70 years. You can't engage in nation building!" Satan says the same thing to us. He says, "If anybody can't do it, it's you!"

Only, he says it like it came from us—"If anybody can't do it, it's me!" That's exactly what he does when we are facing a mountain. He messes with our identity. Like the Jews who were in captivity because of their sin, he reminds us of our failures. "You think you can live in the authority of Christ? What audacity! You know how you have sinned. You can't possibly think Christ is going to honor your attempts to wield His authority with those darkened thoughts and hidden motives in your heart. You are a poor representative of Jesus!" Those are the kinds of lies he whispers (sometimes shouts) in our ears.

2. He attacks our ability. Sanballat asked, "…are they going to restore it for themselves?" (Nehemiah 4:2). He was saying, "The Jews have been an oppressed people. They are beaten down. They do not have the ability or education to rebuild the wall." How many times have we thought those same things about ourselves? *I am not smart enough, or spiritual enough. I can't do it.* We think about the impossibility of the mountain we are facing, and then look at our obvious spiritual weaknesses and think there is no way we can claim authority over that mountain.

> We cannot fight [Satan's] thoughts with our thoughts. We have to fight thoughts with words.

3. He attacks our security. "Can they offer sacrifices?" (Nehemiah 4:2). Sanballat is reminding them of their 70 years of captivity. They were there, according to their prophets, because their God was punishing them. They were a nation guilty of heinous sin. So what makes them think their God will accept them now? Any sacrifice they try to offer will be too late. I can hear the enemy saying the same thing to us. "You have failed so completely, God will never accept you."

4. He attacks our faith. "Can they finish in a day?" (Nehemiah 4:2). Building a wall around the city was an enormous project, especially for displaced refugees who had spent their lives as slaves.

How could they ever hope to organize an engineering feat like this? Satan tries to tell us our plans are too unrealistic, too big. "God may do something like that for others, but He will not do it for you." Only, we hear—*He won't do it for me.*

5. He emphasizes the impossibility. "Can they revive the stones from the dusty rubble even the burned ones?" (Nehemiah 4:2). The enemy wants us to feel like everything is too broken and burned. It would take too long to make things right. Too much damage has been done. It is impossible to bring any good out of this situation. Those are the things he whispers in our ears.

6. He attacks our stability. "If a fox should jump on it, he would break their stone wall down!" (Nehemiah 4:3). In other words, whatever you do to try to fix the situation, will not last. In a short while, everything will be just the way it was. Everything you try to rebuild will crumble, because people do not really change.

> In the prayer of command, we speak directly to the mountain. In the prayer of request, we ask God. It's important we don't mix up these two.

Many hear voices in their head. They think either it is normal, or that they are going crazy. If we hear voices, we are not alone. It is more common than we realize, because the battle is in the mind. The enemy will work over time talking to us about our mountain. He doesn't talk out loud. The attack is in our minds. However—and this is really important—we cannot fight back in our minds. We cannot fight his thoughts with our thoughts. We have to fight thoughts with words. That's why Jesus said to speak to our mountain. There are some important things to keep in mind when speaking to our mountain.

1. Speaking to our mountain is not a magic force. Some people incorrectly think our confession of faith, or speaking to the mountain,

is some kind of magical force. Our words alone have no power. Our faith is in God, not our words. When Jesus told his disciples to have faith, He completed the statement with, "Have faith in God." (Mark 11:22). Our faith is not in our words, or in ourselves. Our faith does not rest on the church. Our faith is in God alone. Bob George in his book, *Classic Christianity*, talks about this by referring to a clutch in a car.[3] When someone is admiring a powerful car they don't say, "Wow! What a clutch!" They admire the engine, the body style, the wheels, the paint job, but not the clutch. There's no power in the clutch. It serves only to connect the power of the engine to the drive train. Faith is the same way. It does not possess the power. Faith is simply the means of connecting the power of God to our situation.

2. Before speaking to our mountain, we have to determine if we should pray a prayer of command or a prayer of request. There are two different kinds of prayers mentioned in Jesus' teaching. He speaks about commanding the mountain to move. "Truly I say to you, whoever says to this mountain, 'Be taken up and cast into the sea'…" (Mark 11:23a). Here the person is told to speak directly to the mountain—to command it to be cast into the sea. But then in verse 24 Jesus says, "Therefore I say to you, all things for which you pray and ask, believe that you have received them, and they will be granted you." (Mark 11:24). In this verse, Jesus referred to making a request.

In the prayer of command, we speak directly to the mountain. In the prayer of request, we ask God. It's important we don't mix up these two. We cannot command God to do anything. We must ask Him. Likewise, we cannot ask our mountain to be removed. We must command it to move. The question is, how do we know when we need to pray a prayer of command, or a prayer of request? I believe we make the distinction by determining if the thing we are praying about involves a human will.

We have no authority over another human will. When dealing with a situation that involves another person, we must offer a prayer of request to God. For example, if we are praying for the salvation of another we cannot command their unbelief to be cast into the sea. They must exercise their will to choose. Even God will not force someone against his or her will to believe. In that case, we ask God to open their eyes to the gospel.

An example from scripture would be in Matthew's gospel where Jesus spoke about workers for the harvest. "Seeing the people, He felt compassion for them, because they were distressed and dispirited like sheep without a shepherd. Then He said to His disciples, 'The harvest is plentiful, but the workers are few. Therefore beseech the Lord of the harvest to send out workers into His harvest.'" (Matthew 9:36-38). Jesus said to ask the Father to send workers into the harvest. We are not to command workers in the name of Jesus. We are to ask God to call them. Then they will have to respond to God's call by their own volition. That is because God will not force someone against his or her own will.

But then there are times when we are dealing with non-persons—spiritual entities, situations, and circumstances. These are the times when we would use a prayer of command. Jesus rebuked the wind and the waves. He rebuked the fever in Peter's mother-in-law. He commanded demons to leave their hosts. For example, if someone was struggling with a spirit of fear, we can command the fear to be cast away. There may be times when we have to pray both ways.

Let's say a friend is in great debt and asks us to pray for them. We can command their debt to be cast into the sea. That's an appropriate prayer. However, that is not enough. Perhaps they are in debt because they have mismanaged their finances. In that case, all the commanding in the world won't make a difference. They have a free will and so we must also ask God to open their eyes to His financial principles, and make them hungrier for freedom, than they are for the things they can purchase. This is not an exact science, but we must seek the Lord's discernment so that we know how to pray appropriately. But when it is time to speak, we must command the mountain to move. We must speak to it if we hope to see a change.

4
The Scope of Faith

The heart of Jesus' teaching is in verses 23 and 24. "Truly I say to you, whoever says to this mountain, 'Be taken up and cast into the sea,' and does not doubt in his heart, but believes that what he says is going to happen, it will be granted him. Therefore I say to you, all things for which you pray and ask, believe that you have received them, and they will be granted you." (Mark 11:23-24). Jesus made some radical claims in this passage.

First, He said this teaching applies to everyone, not just apostles, prophets or His disciples. He said, "…whoever says to this mountain…" That means this teaching is for us. More impressive, He said that we can move mountains. Have you paused to consider the implications of that? What mountains are you facing? Perhaps it's financial, disease, addiction, family conflict, or marriage troubles. While everyone's mountain (problem) is different, the promise to cast it into the sea is the same. Any of us can do it. Candidly, it seems too good to be true. That's probably why Jesus began His teaching with a word of assurance. Notice He prefaced His lesson by saying, "Truly I say to you…" He was emphasizing that this is the Word of Christ to us. He said it twice. In verse 23 he said, "Truly I say to you…" Again in verse 24 He said, "Therefore I say to you..." Jesus was placing all His authority behind those two statements. In fact, the word truly was Jesus' way of saying He guarantees that what He is teaching is true.

We believe everything Jesus said was true, so why add this statement? This teaching was not any truer than anything else He said, but He knows the promise is so expansive, that we will require reassurance. Read His statement again, "Therefore I say to you, all things for which you pray and ask, believe that you have received them, and they will be granted you." (Mark 11:24). The heart of that statement is, "…all things for which you pray and ask, they will be granted you." Think of the enormity of that—all things! The promise is even more amazing when we consider other Scriptures that tell us God cannot lie.

"God is not a man, that He should lie." (Numbers 23:19). "It is impossible for God to lie." (Hebrews 6:18). Think of it this way: in Psalm 15 David asks two important questions. "O Lord, who may abide in Your tent? Who may dwell on Your holy hill?" (Psalm 15:1). God answers the questions by listing 11 characteristics. Notice the 9th characteristic in v.4b—"...he swears to his own hurt and does not change." That means when they give their word, they keep it, even when it hurts.

Think of poor Jephthah, one of the men who delivered Israel from oppression. The book of Judges tells us he was a great warrior, but had been rejected by his people, because he was the son of a harlot. However, when the Ammonites threatened Israel, they turned to him and asked him to lead them in battle. At first he refused. Why should he help them when they rejected him? But they promised to make him chief over them if he would consent. He agreed.

After seeing what he was up against, he made a vow to God that if God would give him victory, upon returning home, he would sacrifice the first thing that came out of his house. That sounds risky, but often animals were kept in the home. Perhaps he thought a lamb would come out first.

To his horror, his daughter was the first to come out and greet him. He tore his clothes in anguish, but kept his word. Some commentators believe he didn't kill her, but offered her to temple service where she would remain a virgin priestess for the rest of her life. She was his only child and therefore, his family line would end with him.

Being born of a harlot, having a family would have been of extreme importance in erasing the stain that had plagued him with his scandalous birth. Regardless the cost, Jephthah kept his word. He sacrificed his one and only child in spite of the loss it cost him. He swore to his own hurt and did not change.

God, through the writings of David, commended one who makes a promise and keeps it, even when it hurts. If God expects that of us, how much more will He be required to live according to His own standard? When God goes on record and gives His word, He keeps it, even when it brings Him pain. He will stand by His promise for His word is on display. It is binding.

The most powerful name in all creation is Jesus. "For this reason also, God highly exalted Him, and bestowed on Him the name which is above every name, so that at the name of Jesus every knee will bow, of those who are in heaven and on earth and under the earth, and that every tongue will confess that Jesus Christ is Lord, to the glory of God the Father." (Philippians 2:9-11). There is no greater name than Jesus, but God places His word above His name! "You have magnified Your word above all Your name!" (Psalm 138:2 Amplified Bible). God's word is even more important to Him than His name, because His name is a handle He has given us to describe Him, but His word is the very expression of his heart, will and mind. So when Jesus makes a statement like this—"…all things for which you pray and ask, they will be granted you…"—His very reputation and integrity are on the line. That's why He loves it when we stand on His word and hold Him to it.

When Jesus made this promise He said we would receive answers for "all things" for which we pray and ask (Mark 11:24). I don't have to tell you, but sometimes I have to remind myself that all means all. It means there are no exceptions or limitations. But when we think about what Jesus is saying it seems too big. That's one of the reasons Jesus prefaced His statement with the word "truly." He knew we would have trouble with the enormity of the statement. Does this mean that if we ask in faith we can be guaranteed to win the lottery next week? No. We always have to interpret Scripture with Scripture.

Last year we purchased a new home in Ohio. One of the first things we intended to do once we moved in was build a privacy fence. There had originally been a restriction on the homeowners in that neighborhood that prohibited the owners from building fences (unless you had a pool) or sheds. The previous owner told us that the covenant had expired in 2012 so we were free to build if we wanted. That was important to us because we have a dog and wanted him to be able to run in the back yard. When we sought the building permit we were denied. The city officials read the covenant and interpreted the language to mean the restrictions would automatically renew in 2012.

Not to be deterred, we investigated any loopholes we could find. Honestly, had we known we couldn't build, we would never have bought the home. Finally, we got the city to allow us to build if we could get a petition signed by our neighbors. My wife, Marcia, is much more likable than me, so I asked her if she would be willing to go around with a clipboard and petition. She agreed. She is an extreme people person and loved the opportunity to meet the neighbors. She is a friend with a number of the women in our neighborhood now.

At first, folks were resistant, because it was the time of the Presidential elections and Trump was running against Clinton. Some thought she was a political activist canvassing the neighborhood for votes. However, she eventually got enough names signed to get approval for the fence. I owe her for that one!

Our dog, Wally, was thrilled when we let him in the backyard without a leash. He ran around and around. He was free to run, sniff and do his business anywhere he wanted, as long as he stayed within the boundaries of the fence. He had total freedom within prescribed limits.

There are boundaries with God. Jesus said we can ask for all things, but within the boundaries He has set. God clearly defines those boundaries in Scripture. "This is the confidence which we have before Him, that, if we ask anything according to His will, He hears us. And if we know that He hears us in whatever we ask, we know that we have the requests which we have asked from Him." (1 John 5:14-15). If we ask God anything within the boundaries of His will, there is no limit to what we can ask.

Already I can hear two questions. First, how do we know what the will of God is? And second, doesn't that seem restrictive, and perhaps a bit convenient? If the answer doesn't come, we can simply say it must not have been God's will. So we ask for whatever we want and hope the cosmic roulette wheel lands on "God's will." If we prayed like that, there would be no confidence, just a lot of hoping and guessing.

We often blame unanswered prayer on God. My friend wasn't healed, so it must not have been God's will. My sister got cancer, so it must have been God's will. God gets blamed for a lot of stuff He doesn't do. There are boundaries to His will, but they are much larger than we perhaps may think.

First, we need to understand that God is on our side. He thinks far better of us than we do ourselves. That's because He sees us in Christ. Paul wrote, "He made Him who knew no sin to be sin on our behalf, so that we might become the righteousness of God in Him." (2 Corinthians 5:21). Paul said there was an amazing exchange that took place at the cross. He took on all of our sin and gave us His righteousness. That means the Father sees us through the lens of His Son's perfections.

Zephaniah says He sings over us. "The Lord your God is with you, the Mighty Warrior who saves. He will take great delight in you; in His love He will no longer rebuke you, but will rejoice over you with singing." (Zephaniah 3:17 NIV). He rejoices over the thought of you. You are His prize creation and He has great plans for you. "For we are His workmanship, created in Christ Jesus for good works, which God prepared beforehand so that we would walk in them." (Ephesians 2:10).

When we think of God's will for us we have to broaden our view. God wants us to live with bigger expectations because it magnifies Him. In fact, when we believe too small it insults Him. A father came to Jesus with a sick child. He pleaded with Jesus to heal the boy. In his plea he made a statement that offended Jesus. The boy was demon possessed. Explaining the situation, that man said, "It has often thrown him both into the fire and into the water to destroy him. But if You can do anything, take pity on us and help us!" (Mark 9:22).

Jesus repeated back what the man said in the form of a question. "And Jesus said to him, 'If You can?' All things are possible to him who believes." I imagine Jesus emphasized the word if. "*If* You can? What do you mean *if*? Of course I can!" I believe that was the gist of what Jesus was saying. He then healed the boy.

Granted our limitations may not be on the Lord's ability. We may fully agree that Jesus can do anything if He wills it. Our struggle is with whether or not He wants to grant the request. I find it interesting that every time Jesus confronted someone who was sick, He felt compassion for them. He never turned an indifferent eye. Even if someone isn't healed, we know that God feels compassion, for as I said in my first book, God is identical to Jesus. They are exactly alike.

In the record of the Kings, a king was seeking a promise from God via His prophet. The prophet gave the instruction.

When Elisha became sick with the illness of which he was to die, Joash the king of Israel came down to him and wept over him and said, "My father, my father, the chariots of Israel and its horsemen!" Elisha said to him, "Take a bow and arrows." So he took a bow and arrows. Then he said to the king of Israel, "Put your hand on the bow." And he put his hand on it, then Elisha laid his hands on the king's hands. He said, "Open the window toward the east," and he opened it. Then Elisha said, "Shoot!" And he shot. And he said, "The Lord's arrow of victory, even the arrow of victory over Aram; for you will defeat the Arameans at Aphek until you have destroyed them." Then he said, "Take the arrows," and he took them. And he said to the king of Israel, "Strike the ground," and he struck it three times and stopped. So the man of God was angry with him and said, "You should have struck five or six times, then you would have struck Aram until you would have destroyed it. But now you shall strike Aram only three times." (2 Kings 13:14-19).

God desires more for us than we realize. There are limitations within His set boundaries, but that fenced in area is much larger than we may think. There is a verse I like to call the fence line of God's will. "For as many as are the promises of God, in Him they are yes; therefore also through Him is our Amen to the glory of God through us." (2 Corinthians 1:20). I want to unpack this powerful verse. Paul begins by saying, "For as many as are the promises of God…" That's another way of saying all the promises of God. As many as there are is all-inclusive. So Paul is saying that no matter how may promises God has made, His answer to each is yes. "For as many as are the promises of God (that means all of them), in Him they are yes." However, be sure and notice there is a condition. The promises are yes "in Him." That is referring to Jesus. We could re-read it this way: "For all the promises God has made, in Jesus, His answer is yes." That means if we come to God and claim His promises in the name of Jesus, then the answer is yes. Now stay with me, because I am not teaching a "name it-claim it" theology. We have to understand when we ask something in the name of Jesus we are asking for something as if it were Jesus who was asking for it. In other words, we are asking as His representative. In order to accurately represent Him, we have to ask according to His will. So Paul is saying every promise we claim, if it is in the will of Jesus, then God's answer is yes. But the verse says more. It also says, "through Him (Jesus) is our amen." Amen is our response. It means let it be so. It is a declaration of faith. When God says yes, we respond with amen and it is settled. Our declaration is a verbal response, a confession of faith.

When Israel was commanded to go into Canaan and possess the land, they were marching into territory God had already given them. It was their inheritance, but they still had to go in and possess it. They had to possess their possessions. They had to dispossess the current occupiers and take up residence. Our verbal declaration of "Amen" is our way of possessing our possessions. It's how we place our feet in Canaan. Every promise within the will of God is our possession, but we have to claim it. We have to speak to the fig tree. The thing that is remarkable to me is that Paul referred to all the promises of God. Even the Old Testament promises are ours, for we are the seed of Abraham and have inherited all the promises made to him and his seed.

> Now the promises were spoken to Abraham and to his seed. He does not say, "And to seeds," as referring to many, but rather to one, "And to your seed," that is, Christ. What I am saying is this: the Law, which came four hundred and thirty years later, does not invalidate a covenant previously ratified by God, so as to nullify the promise. For if the inheritance is based on law, it is no longer based on a promise; but God has granted it to Abraham by means of a promise... And if you belong to Christ, then you are Abraham's descendants, heirs according to promise. (Galatians 3:16-18, 29).

Does that really mean we can claim all the promises of God? Yes, and no. There are some specific promises we can't claim, and most likely would not want to: like the promise to Sarah that she would get pregnant and have a baby at the age of 90. Any women want to go for that? Behind that specific promise, however, there is a broader promise. God was promising the fulfillment of His purposes in Sarah and Abraham's life. That is a type of promise we can claim. For example, there are many promises made specifically to the nation of

Israel. There is one that is directed solely to the nation, but I often hear people claim the promise personally. Maybe you have claimed this promise: "'For I know the plans that I have for you,' declares the Lord, 'plans for welfare and not for calamity to give you a future and a hope.'" (Jeremiah 29:11). If we read this verse in its proper context, it is clear it is an exclusive word to Israel.

> For thus says the Lord, "When seventy years have been completed for Babylon, I will visit you and fulfill My good word to you, to bring you back to this place. For I know the plans that I have for you," declares the Lord, "plans for welfare and not for calamity to give you a future and a hope. Then you will call upon Me and come and pray to Me, and I will listen to you. You will seek Me and find Me when you search for Me with all your heart. I will be found by you," declares the Lord, "and I will restore your fortunes and will gather you from all the nations and from all the places where I have driven you," declares the Lord, "and I will bring you back to the place from where I sent you into exile." (Jeremiah 29:10-14).

This is a promise to restore scattered Israel back to her homeland. Many interpret it as a promise about their own personal future, but God is speaking here about a great miracle that took place under the leadership of both Ezra and Nehemiah, when the Israelites came back into their land. We also see an echo of fulfillment when they came into their land again in 1948.

Is it then proper to claim this promise for our personal lives? Yes, and no. No, we cannot claim what is specifically stated. But yes, we can extract the principle and claim that. We can extract from that promise universal principles that are ours by inheritance. Let me walk through this to unpack what I mean. God knows the beginning from the end. With that knowledge, He has plans for you that have been made before the beginning of creation (Ephesians 1:4; 2:10). God's plans reflect His will. God's will reflects His nature. God's nature is good; therefore, His plans are always good. God would not plan evil for you. Therefore, God's plans for you are good. Good, however, refers to that which glorifies God (See Romans 8:28-29). That means God's plans are for you to bring glory to God, which results in the greatest fulfillment of our existence. Based on that logic, we can claim Jeremiah 29:11.

Here's another thing to consider with God's promises: there are thousands of them. We can't claim every one of them, at least, not all at once. They are all available to us, but we have to be able to discern when God is saying a specific promise is to be applied to our specific situation. I do not believe the Bible is a dead document. The Holy Spirit can breathe on a passage and make it come alive to our immediate situation. That means when considering the promises of God—and the entire Scripture for that matter—we have to discern between the Logos of God and the Rhema of God. Let me explain what I mean. Hebrews 4:12 says, "For the word of God is living and active and sharper than any two-edged sword, and piercing as far as the division of soul and spirit, of both joints and marrow, and able to judge the thoughts and intentions of the heart." The term for "word" is the Greek word *logos*, which commonly indicates the expression of a complete idea. It is used in referring to the Holy Scriptures. But also, John describes Jesus as "the Logos", for He is the living expression of God's word (John 1:1). So the Logos is God's completed word. Jesus is the Logos, but the Bible we hold in our hands is also the Logos.

> "Faith does not operate in the realm of the possible. There is no glory for God in that which is humanly possible. Faith begins where man's power ends."
> — George Muller

The other term Scripture uses to describe itself is *rhema*. Strong's Concordance defines this word as "an utterance (individually, collectively or specially)."[4] While this refers to Scripture, it is generally used to describe the spoken word. For example, we see the term used in Ephesians. "And take the helmet of salvation, and the sword of the Spirit, which is the **word** of God." (Ephesians 6:17 emphasis added). The term translated "word" is *rhema*. Paul is saying the sword of the Spirit is the *rhema* of God. Paul is telling us, in this verse, to use the word of God as a weapon. He is also telling us that the Holy Spirit is involved in the wielding of that weapon, for it is "the sword **of the Spirit**."

Jesus said the Holy Spirit would bring to our mind all that Christ had taught us. That means when in battle, we have to specifically apply a portion of the word to our immediate situation—as Jesus did in the wilderness. Each time Jesus responded to Satan's attack, He answered with a quotation from the Bible. (Matthew 4:1-11). The Holy Spirit brings a Scripture to mind in the moment of need. When that specific word is applied, it is spoken, for we wield the word like a sword by declaring it. The Holy Spirit makes that word come alive for that specific situation. At that moment, that word becomes a *rhema* word of God for us. God takes from the *logos*—the whole Bible—and applies a specific *rhema*, a specific passage from the Scriptures for our immediate situation.

Therefore, when we think of the promises of God: the Holy Spirit will take all the promises of God and make a specific one alive for us at the needed moment. When we have that promise, we know God's will in that matter. When we think about the borders of God's will, we must remember God's fence line is as big as His promises in Scripture. That is why it is imperative we know the Scriptures so we are ready to receive the *rhema* of God when needed. God cannot withdraw from our spiritual bank account until we first make a deposit.

The mountain we face may seem insurmountable, but think of God's vantage point. If you have ever had the privilege of hiking in the

Rocky Mountains you know how impassable they appear. I once took the cog railway to the top of Pike's Peak in Colorado. When standing at the top, you can look in any direction and see an endless series of white-capped peaks that extend to the horizon. When standing there I wondered how the early settlers ever got through. It seems endless. From the base the mountains shoot so high into the sky, the clouds eat them. They are jagged and huge. Yet if you have ever seen a photograph of the surface of the earth from outer space, it appears to be a smooth, curved surface. There appears to be no mountains, hills or bumps. It is smooth. From our perspective, the mountains of our lives are overwhelming, but from God's perspective, they are nothing. Zerubbabel had an impossible task of rebuilding the Jewish Temple. It was truly an impassable mountain. The prophet Zechariah said Zerubbabel would not accomplish the project by strength or might, but by the Spirit of the Lord. When speaking his word of encouragement to Zerubbabel he said, "What are you, O great mountain? Before Zerubbabel you will become a plain." (Zechariah 4:7). That's how God looks at our mountains. [5]

5
The Enemy of Faith

Jesus said our mountains could be cast into the sea. There is, however, a condition placed on the promise. "Truly I say to you, whoever says to this mountain, 'Be taken up and cast into the sea,' and does not doubt in his heart, but believes that what he says is going to happen, it will be granted him." (Mark 11:23). We have to speak to our mountain without doubt. The word for doubt in the Greek is revealing. It is the word, *diakrino*. It is made from two Greek words—*dia* meaning "among many", and *krino*, which means, "to decide". Literally, it means, "to decide among many." It is to judge between two things: to vacillate between options. Think of an oscillating fan that keeps swinging back and forth. Picture someone walking on a path. They come to a fork in the road. They start to walk down the left fork, but quickly change their mind and turn down the right fork. Then, just as they start down the right path, they second-guess themselves and turn back to the left—back and forth, like the fan, they can't decide. That's what it means to doubt.

> God's actions always occur in the root first. If we refuse to doubt at the root, it will eventually manifest in the branches.

Jesus said when we command our problem to be cast into the sea we cannot doubt; we cannot vacillate between the two. My question is: What two things can we not vacillate between? What are the two possible paths we can walk down? Remember, the disciples were standing in front of a tree. The day before, when Jesus cursed the tree, the roots immediately died, but were invisible to the eye. Only after 24 hours did the disciples see the death that was in the roots spread into the branches. We exercise doubt when we command something in faith, and believe it is done in the realm of the spirit (the root), but then doubt when we don't see it manifest in the realm of the flesh (the branches). Jesus said when we speak to the root of the tree, we must believe we have received. We must not look at the branches and say, "God didn't answer." If the disciples had made a judgment the day before, they would have said Jesus' words had no effect on the tree. At that point they would have believed what they saw, rather than what they heard Jesus say. God's actions always occur in the root first. If we refuse to doubt at the root, it will eventually manifest in the branches.

Peter learned this when he walked on the water. He walked toward Jesus, but then looked at the waves and wind and began to sink. When Jesus took his hand He asked, "Why did you doubt". He used the same word (*diakrino*) as is used in our story. Peter vacillated. He went back and forth between Jesus' word to him that he could walk on water, and the impending peril of the waves. We must not believe the circumstances that surround us. They are like waves that will crash in on our lives. The enemy uses them to whisper in our ears, "You're going to sink". Instead, we must believe Christ's word. If He calls us to walk on the water, then we can no matter what the waves say. We cannot allow circumstances to manipulate our faith. We often speak to the problem, then look at the leaves and think to ourselves, *it is still there. It didn't work.* Many will not believe unless they can see. Jesus said unless you believe you will not see.

> Doubt always attacks the interim between the root and the branches. We believe it is accomplished in the realm of the spirit and wait for it to manifest in the realm of the flesh. We are spiritually vulnerable during that interval.

Doubt always attacks the interim between the root and the branches. We believe it is accomplished in the realm of the spirit and wait for it to manifest in the realm of the flesh. We are spiritually vulnerable during that interval. Choosing to believe it is done in the root is always a contest between God's word and what we see with our eyes. Doubt lurks in the shadows ready to pounce. And here's the tricky thing about doubt: faith and doubt can exist in the heart at the same time. Peter had doubt in his heart when he looked at the wind and waves and began to sink. But don't miss the fact he had enough faith to start walking on the water. Remember the old scales that were used to weigh goods? The product was placed on one side and the coins were placed on the other. When one side of the scale was pushed down, the other side was lifted up. Some see faith and doubt like that scale. When our faith increases, our doubt decreases; and vice versa. But that's not actually how it works. Belief and unbelief can exist in the heart at the same time.

Jesus encountered a desperate father who pled with Him to heal his son of a demonic infestation. When Jesus questioned the man, he revealed his heart was mixed.

> They brought the boy to Him. When he saw Him, immediately the spirit threw him into a convulsion, and falling to the ground, he began rolling around and foaming at the mouth. And He [Jesus] asked his father, "How long has this been happening to him?" And he said, "From childhood. It has often thrown him both into the fire and into the water to destroy him. But if You can do anything, take pity on us and help us!" And Jesus said to him, "If You can? All things are possible to him who believes." Immediately the boy's father cried out and said, "I do believe; help my unbelief." (Mark 9:20-24).

He believed, but he also struggled with unbelief. The scales were tipped on both sides. The key to believing, and not doubting is not trying to make ourselves believe more. The key is to get rid of the doubt.

Doubt is a huge problem because it offends God's integrity. James tells us that when we encounter various trials (mountains) they will serve to test our faith. "Consider it all joy, my brethren, when you encounter various trials, knowing that the **testing of your faith** produces endurance." (James 1:2-3 emphasis added). One of the results of those trials, when faced properly, is to produce maturity in us. "And let endurance have its perfect result, so that you may be perfect and complete, lacking in nothing." (James 1:4). When we are in the middle of a trial, we often don't know what to do. Recognizing that, James tells us we can ask God for wisdom. "But if any of you lacks wisdom, let him ask of God, who gives to all generously and without reproach, and it will be given to him." (James 1:5). Notice James connects this word of instruction with the previous subject of trials by beginning the verse with the word "but". He is making the connection between trials and our need for wisdom in the middle of them. Wisdom is different than knowledge. Knowledge is information; whereas wisdom is knowing what to do with that information. James says that if we ask God for wisdom, He will give it—generously.

However, there is a condition. "But he must ask in faith without any doubting, for the one who doubts is like the surf of the sea, driven and tossed by the wind. For that man ought not to expect that he will receive anything from the Lord." (James 1:6-7). This passage is speaking again of doubt. And James uses the same word, *diakrino*, which means to vacillate. It refers to shifting between trusting God to give the guidance sought, or depending on self to figure out our own course of action. But James says if we ask for guidance, God will give it, and generously. So when we ask God for wisdom, but then don't trust He will give it, we doubt. But more than that we show we do not trust God to follow through on his word. "For that man ought not to expect that he will receive anything from the Lord, being a double-minded man, unstable in all his ways." (James 1:7-8).

Have you ever been in a situation where someone accused you of something you didn't do, and when you defended yourself, they didn't believe you? I have had that happen. I remember someone accused me of lying. They at least had the guts to say it to my face. The problem was, I didn't have any idea what they were talking about. I hadn't lied about anything. But when I asked them to clarify, they responded by saying, "You know what you did." They accused me of lying, but wouldn't share any details or evidence and I was in the dark as to what they were talking about. I knew at that moment, that no matter what I said, they wouldn't believe me. They did not think I was a person of integrity. It was such an insult. They were judging my heart and motives. It was very offensive. That's what James implies we are doing to God when we ask for wisdom, but then doubt He will give it—even when He promises to give it generously. Doubt is an insult to the character of God.

> During the interim, when we are waiting for the reality of the roots to manifest in the branches, Satan attacks with doubt.

One reason it is so serious, is because doubt is far more than an emotion. It is a spiritual attack. Doubt is not an emotional struggle that we have no control over. Doubt is a spiritual assault from the enemy. Paul wrote about the devil shooting arrows at the shield of faith, "…in addition to all, taking up the shield of faith with which you will be able to extinguish all the flaming arrows of the evil one." (Ephesians 6:16). He attacks our faith with arrows of doubt. During the interim, when we are waiting for the reality of the roots to manifest in the branches, Satan attacks with doubt. During that time, what are we going to trust—God's word of promise, or Satan's word of pessimism? When we pray and believe the answer is given in the root, we are stepping into spiritual warfare. At that point, our battle strategy is not about how to increase our belief, but rather, how to fight off doubt. There are at least four ways we can fight against the attacks of doubt.

1. We fight against doubt by confessing it. When Jesus questioned the man with the demon-possessed son, you could tell He was frustrated. The man pled with Jesus to do something for his boy, saying, "If you can do anything." Jesus responded, "If I can?" Of course He can! But this man was hesitant, tentative. Jesus told him anything was possible if he believed. Then the man openly confessed he did believe, but he also disbelieved—"I do believe, help my unbelief." (Mark 9:24). Jesus may have been frustrated with the man's doubts (and the disciples' as well) but He took pity on him and healed his son. I believe Jesus responded because the man was honest. He confessed his doubts to Christ. We have to do the same. It's important, because the answer to doubt is not ultimately a technique. It is a person, the living Christ. And know this—Jesus wants to help us with our mountains. He asks us to invite Him into the battle to take our hand and walk with us on the water. We still have to do the walking—and fighting—but we can invite Him to join arms with us and He will.

> When we pray and believe the answer is given in the root, we are stepping into spiritual warfare.

2. We fight doubt by the Word of God. When Jesus stood with His disciples by that fig tree, He commanded them to "have faith in God." (Mark 11:22). That command actually reached back to His previous statement the day before when He cursed the tree. Though He was addressing the tree, He knew His disciples were listening when He said, "May no one ever eat fruit from you again!" (Mark 11:14). The next day when Jesus said to have faith in God, He was inferring back to what He had said the day before. They saw a withered tree and were marveling at the sight before them, but the day before they had heard the Lord curse the tree. The moment He said it was the moment the tree died, and should have

been the point at which they marveled. In other words, their faith should have been attached to Jesus' words, rather than the sight of a withered tree. What Jesus said the day before should have been enough to believe without having to see the withered tree. The source of faith is not what we see with our eyes. Instead it is the word of Christ. "So faith comes from hearing, and hearing by the word of Christ." (Romans 10:17). If we are to live by faith and see the reality of God pulled into our physical realm, we will have to learn to depend on the Word of God, rather than what we can see with our eyes.

John the Baptist had made a public declaration that Jesus was the Lamb of God who came to take away the sins of the world (John 1:29). After John's arrest, he too was assaulted with doubt. "Now when John, while imprisoned, heard of the works of Christ, he sent word by his disciples and said to Him, 'Are You the Expected One, or shall we look for someone else?'" Now he had doubts about whether Jesus was the one. John saw the Holy Spirit, in the form of a dove, land on Jesus at His baptism. Jesus said John was the greatest man of the Old Testament dispensation (Matthew 11:11). But in spite of that, John struggled with doubt. If he was attacked at his point of vulnerability, then any of us are susceptible. Jesus' answer to John's disciples is telling. "Jesus answered and said to them, 'Go and report to John what you hear and see: the blind receive sight and the lame walk, the lepers are cleansed and the deaf hear, the dead are raised up, and the poor have the gospel preached to them.'" (Matthew 11:4-5). Jesus answered John's disciples by quoting Scripture. His statements about the blind, lame, deaf and dead, were a direct quote from Isaiah (Isaiah 35:5-6; 61:1). Jesus counter-attacked the assault of doubt by quoting Scripture!

We often brainwash ourselves with negative lies that instill doubt against any hope of change. The person who constantly repeats to him or herself that they are a failure is playing into the devil's hands. They dig deep trenches of doubt across their soul. We can do just the opposite with Scripture. When the attack comes, we can declare the word, out loud, repeatedly to fight off the arrows of doubt. Take the *rhema* word that God's Spirit spoke to your heart when confirming His will concerning the root, and use it as a weapon against the attacks of doubt.

3. We fight doubt by singing praises. Most people enjoy music. It has the power to move us emotionally, but I suspect there is something more to it than that. When King Saul was tormented by a demon, David was brought to court to play his instrument for him. David's playing had a miraculous effect on Saul. "So it came about whenever the evil spirit from God came to Saul, David would take the harp and play it with his hand; and Saul would be refreshed and be well, and the evil spirit would depart from him." (1 Samuel 16:23). When the prophet Elisha was called on to speak a word for God, he asked for music to assist him. "Elisha said, 'As the Lord of hosts lives, before whom I stand, were it not that I regard the presence of Jehoshaphat the king of Judah, I would not look at you nor see you. But now bring me a minstrel.' And it came about, when the minstrel played, that the hand of the Lord came upon him." (2 Kings 3:14-15).

Ludwig van Beethoven is credited with saying, "Music is the mediator between the spiritual and the sensual life."[6] A full-throated praise in the presence of God seems to naturally explode into song. When God created the universe, the angelic host was there to watch and their response was musical. God asked Job, "Where were you when I laid the foundation of the earth? Tell Me, if you have understanding, who set its measurements? Since you know. Or who stretched the line on it? On what were its bases sunk? Or who laid its cornerstone, when the **morning stars sang together** and all the sons of God shouted for joy?" (Job 38:4-7 emphasis added). The morning stars are a reference to the angelic host (Revelation 12:3-4).

Music is a powerful weapon. We see that displayed in bold relief in 2 Chronicles. The Moabites and Ammonites came to war against King Jehoshaphat. Israel was out numbered and out gunned. They were intimidated. The King turned to God in prayer and God instructed him to call out the choir. Chronicles reveals their battle strategy.

> They rose early in the morning and went out to the wilderness of Tekoa; and when they went out, Jehoshaphat stood and said, "Listen to me, O Judah and inhabitants of Jerusalem, put your trust in the Lord your God and you will be established. Put your trust in His prophets and succeed." When he had consulted with the people, he appointed **those who sang to the Lord** and those who praised Him in holy attire, as **they went out before the army** and said, "Give thanks to the Lord, for His lovingkindness is everlasting." **When they began singing and praising, the Lord set ambushes against the sons of Ammon, Moab and Mount Seir**, who had come against Judah; so they were routed. (2 Chronicles 20:20-22 emphasis added).

Something happens in our spirit when we elevate God in song. By the way, I don't mean listening to music. I am talking about using music as a form of prayer. You have to sing it. Years ago, one of the guys I was discipling confided with me that he felt stuck in his spiritual progress. He owned several acres of field and woods, so I advised him to take a hymnal into the field where no one could hear him, and sing to the top of his voice. I told him not to worry about how he sounded, but to fully engage in the music. He followed my instruction and sang as loud as he could for more than an hour. While engaging in this form of prayer, he had a breakthrough. The Spirit of God rested upon him and moved in his spirit in a way he had not experienced before. The Psalms make it clear that music is a weapon against the enemy of God. "Let the godly ones exult in glory; let them sing for joy on their beds. Let the high praises of God be in their mouth, and a two-edged sword in their hand, to execute vengeance on the nations and punishment on the peoples, to bind their kings with chains and their nobles with fetters of iron, to execute on them the judgment written; this is an honor for all His godly ones. Praise the Lord!" (Psalm 149:5-9). Sometimes the best thing to do when doubt assails us is to attack with song.

4. We fight doubt by fasting. When Jesus conducted His debrief with His disciples after casting the demon out of the boy (Matthew 17), He told them the key was fasting. "But this kind does not go out but by prayer and fasting." (Matthew 17:21). Granted, some manuscripts don't include this statement, but the parallel account in Mark 9 makes the same statement, and is undisputed in the manuscripts. Why was prayer and fasting necessary to deal with this demon? Was he an especially powerful spirit? Whether he was or not should make no difference since they were operating under the authority of Christ and His power rules over all. Perhaps a clue comes from Jesus' question to the father of the child. "They brought the boy to Him. When he saw Him, immediately the spirit threw him into a convulsion, and falling to the ground,

> Fasting positions us to disregard the voices of the flesh and instead, listen to the voice of God's Spirit.

he began rolling around and foaming at the mouth. And He [Jesus] asked his father, 'How long has this been happening to him?' And he said, 'From childhood.'" (Mark 9:20-21).

This boy had been overtaken by the demon many times. It held such sway over him, that it literally was able to pick the child up and cast him into a fire. To hold that level of possession over a child indicates there must have been some doors opened to the spirit world in that family. The boy foamed at the mouth, and was completely overtaken. Something else was controlling him. The disciples had encountered demon-possessed people before (Luke 10:17). But perhaps this case was different. They saw manifestations they hadn't seen before. Of course they saw the man named Legion who had hundreds of demons in him, and was so strong he broke his chains

(Luke 8:26-39). But Jesus dealt with him. This seems to have been the first time they tried to confront a demon who exhibited such dramatic manifestations. The foaming of the mouth, the throwing into the fire—all appeared like the wind and waves that caused Peter to doubt when walking on the sea.

We are so dominated by our senses that we believe what we see with our eyes of flesh more than what we see with the eyes of faith. The disciples had Christ's authority, but Satan deceived them into thinking this demon's power was greater than what they possessed. Their flesh lied to them. They listened to what their ears heard and believed what their eyes saw. Fasting and prayer are vital because they break the flesh's hold on us so we become more attuned to the spiritual realm. Fasting positions us to disregard the voices of the flesh and instead, listen to the voice of God's Spirit. It does not earn us extra points with God, but it trains us to pay no heed to the flesh so we can overcome doubt.

6
Important Steps When Facing A Mountain

There are some important questions we need to answer when dealing with mountains and roots. Why is there often a delay between the assurance something is answered in the root, and the actual manifestation of it in the branches? Also, are there ever times when we believe at the root, but the answer never manifests in the branches? Are there things that can keep our mountains from plunging into the sea? When people hear this teaching, they often have objections. Many of the objections are embedded in the questions just asked. We need to address them, and I will. However, before diving into those important issues, I believe it necessary to recap the steps unfolded thus far. If we could systematize our approach to the mountain, what would it look like? I will walk us through a step-by-step approach. However, these steps are not necessarily sequential, but they are important.

When facing a mountain the first thing we need to do is confirm God's will in the matter. Praying for the mountain to be moved and believing for the branches to whither, is not about manipulating the Spirit to get what we want. The first responsibility in prayer is to understand God's will. "This is the confidence which we have before Him, that, if we ask anything according to His will, He hears us. And if we know that He hears us in whatever we ask, we know that we have the requests which we have asked from Him." (1 John 5:14-15). We cannot pray a prayer of faith unless we know it is God's will. Our first order of business when interceding or petitioning God is to spend time searching His Word and listening to the voice of His Spirit to discern His leading. I have often taught that when praying we need to imagine ourselves standing in a rowboat. Picture yourself in the boat, ten or twelve feet away from the dock. You have a rope in your hand, and you throw it around the post at the end of the dock. You then begin to pull. When that happens, are you pulling the dock to you, or are you pulling yourself to the dock? The boat is our will. The dock is God's will. Prayer is pulling the rope. The purpose is to align ourselves with God's will, not to try and move Him to ours.

The second thing we need to do, which is really connected to the first, is to discover God's promise for our need in the Scriptures. As we meditate on and pray over the Scriptures, we are seeking confirmation from the Holy Spirit that the passage He highlights to us is His word for us in this situation. It is important we allow the Lord to direct us to the appropriate promise. We can't just randomly select the promise we want. We must listen for His leading as we pray and search the Scriptures. How this happens is as much art as it is science. It is one of those things that you know it when it happens. Have you ever been reading the Bible and a verse you have read a hundred times before jumps off the page and knocks you in the head? It's like that. The one weakness I have in this regard is I have to be honest with myself and make sure I have surrendered my agenda before seeking God's direction. Otherwise it is easy to interpret everything through the lens of what I want. When the Holy Spirit does confirm the Word to us, it builds our faith to appropriate that promise (Romans 10:17).

> Claiming our promise is the equivalent to stepping on ground God has given.

Once we discover and settle on God's promise, we need to investigate if there are any conditions attached to the promise. God's promises are often conditional. God says, "I will do this…if you do that." If the promise has conditions attached to it, we must keep them or God will not fulfill the promise. Exodus 15:26 is a clear example. When God established His laws among Israelites, He promised freedom from disease. However, they had to obey His ways or the promise was null and void. "And He said, 'If you will give earnest heed to the voice of the Lord your God, and do what is right in His sight, and give ear to His commandments, and keep all His statutes, I will put none of the diseases on you which I have put on the Egyptians; for I, the Lord, am your healer.'" (Exodus 15:26). As you continue to read the Exodus story you discover God's Laws included instruction about eating clean food and proper sanitation practices. If Israel disregarded God's direction in those matters, then they would be susceptible to disease.

> I am concerned however, that we have been so cautious about using our words like a magic formula that we have shied away from the power of confession. Our words don't create reality, but they are important because they reveal what is in our heart.

Once we have established the will and promise of God, and have seen clearly any conditions attached to it, we are to claim the promise as our own. Let me reiterate, we can only claim a promise once we know it is God's will. But when God has given us a promise we must claim it. Just like Israel when entering to conquer the Promised Land, we must possess our possessions. "Every place on which the sole of your foot treads, I have given it to you, just as I spoke to Moses." (Joshua 1:3). Claiming our promise is the equivalent to stepping on ground God has given.

Declaring what we believe out loud is vital because of the power of our confession. "That if you confess with your mouth Jesus as Lord, and believe in your heart that God raised Him from the dead, you will be saved; for with the heart a person believes, resulting in righteousness, and with the mouth he confesses, resulting in salvation." (Romans 10:9-10). Notice in verse 10 we see the order of the pattern. It starts in the heart with belief, but then it must also be expressed through the mouth. Granted this verse is dealing with salvation, but if it is important for that, then how much more for answered prayer.

There is a logical reason why confession with our mouths is important. I will admit that some have gotten off track at this point and have tried to say that our words have power; like they are magic. They say they are containers of power and can create reality. That's an extreme view, and I believe an unbiblical one as well. Our words are powerful. A word of encouragement spoken at the right moment can change a life. But words are not creative forces. That is reserved for God alone. "By the word of the Lord the heavens were made, and by the breath of His mouth all their host." (Psalm 33:6). We do not have that power. Only God does. I am concerned however, that we have been so cautious about using our words like a magic formula that we have shied away from the power of confession. Our words don't create reality, but they are important because they reveal what is in our heart. "For the mouth speaks out of that which fills the heart." (Matthew 12:34b). Our words demonstrate what we truly believe. If we believe it, we will say it, and belief is everything. "For whatever is born of God overcomes the world; and **this is the victory that has overcome the world—our faith**." (1 John 5:4b emphasis added).

> Thus the pattern: God promises, we believe, we take the risk to act on that belief, and then God acts.

Another thing we must be careful to do is act on our faith. James says, "But someone may well say, 'You have faith and I have works; show me your faith without the works, and I will show you my faith by my works.'" (James 2:18). Real faith requires action. If we really believe something, we will act the way we believe. The act of faith often involves risk. The Jordan River was at flood stage when Israel entered the Promised Land. God commanded the priests to lead the procession. They were to carry the Ark of the Covenant across the raging river. They were assured that river would not sweep them away. Stepping into a fast current, while carrying a heavy golden box on poles without losing your balance is challenge enough. But in addition there was the threat that if anyone stumbled and accidently touched the ark they would die. Joshua reassured them the river would stop flowing after they took their first step into the water. Thus the pattern: God promises, we believe, we take the risk to act on that belief, and then God acts.

I remember the first time the Lord taught me this principle. I was again walking in my favorite prayer closet, Mantle Lake Park. I was meditating on a passage of Scripture. I had been praying over a youth rally we were planning to host at our church. As I prayed, the Spirit of God impressed on my heart that 30 people were going to give their lives to the Lord during that rally. I began to rejoice and give praise to God while walking on that trail. I can remember, just as clear as if it were yesterday, I sensed the Lord direct me to share that promise with my congregation. I remember arguing with God, *But Lord, I can't share that. What if it doesn't happen? What will come of my credibility? The people will doubt my spiritual discernment and then I won't be able to lead them.* Isn't it funny how we try to argue with God? There was no mistaking it, God wanted me to share it with the congregation. If I really believed, I had to step into the water first. That next Sunday I shared what I had sensed in prayer. Everyone clapped with excitement. We anticipated that God was going to do something wonderful.

I celebrated with them, but then after the service, went into desperate prayer. Our little church was running 150 people and we had a very small youth group. To see 30 saved would be a miracle in deed. The night of the rally people arrived in droves. Van after van, car after car arrived in our little parking lot. I had never seen our little sanctuary so crowded. We counted 470 people in a sanctuary that was full at 175. There was literally no place to walk in the room. It was wall-to-wall people with the front seats so close to the stage that people's knees were bumping the platform.

When it was time for the guest speaker to preach, I introduced him and then left the auditorium. He knew what we had announced and he planned to give an invitation at the end of the service. I pulled a chair into the middle of the room next to the sanctuary and dropped to my knees. I had one thing in mind, thirty people had better respond to the invitation. I prayed fervently during the entire sermon. I would like to say I prayed with great faith, but it was more like desperation. When the invitation was given no one could come forward for there was literally no room for anyone to walk and no place for anyone to kneel to pray. The speaker had those who chose to accept Christ that night, stand. That night exactly 30 people stood to pray and receive Christ. It was a lesson to my people and me. Faith involves risk, but God will empower our choice of obedience.

> When Jesus set up the object lesson, He intentionally built a gap between His spoken word and the withered branches. He could have made the branches wilt instantly, but He didn't, because He set it up to help us understand the nature of prayer.

Another step is to continue to pray. Once we have confirmed it is done in the root, we are to keep praying. However, our prayer at this point is different in nature than before. We discern God's will; pray a prayer of request or declaration, but once it is settled in the root, we shift our focus. Our prayer moves from request to thanksgiving. Once it's settled in the roots, we do not need to ask again, but we do need to fight off the attacks of doubt. Thanksgiving is the key. If we believe we already have it in the root, then why ask for it again? Israel did not need to ask for the Promised

Land. It was already theirs. They needed to possess it. When I asked the church to pray for my migraine headaches (mentioned in chapter 1) I made it clear I did not want them to ask God to heal me. I had His promise He had already healed me. It was done in the root. I was waiting for it to manifest in the branches. Instead, I instructed them to give thanks to God for the healing was already settled. Paul instructed us to bring our requests with thanksgiving. "Be anxious for nothing, but in everything by prayer and supplication **with thanksgiving** let your requests be made known to God." (Philippians 4:6 emphasis added). If it seems to take a long time for the answer to manifest in the branches, we need to inquire if the delay is part of His plan, or our own doing. I will deal with that at length in another chapter.

It is important in this process to wait patiently. Although we do not want any more delay between the roots and branches than necessary, it seems that is the norm. In fact, when Jesus set up the object lesson, He intentionally built a gap between His spoken word and the withered branches. He could have made the branches wilt instantly, but He didn't, because He set it up to help us understand the nature of prayer. And in most cases there is a delay.

> Faith brings the inherited promise into manifestation but patience is also necessary because of the normal delay between the roots and the branches.

The author to Hebrews tells us to be "imitators of those who through **faith and patience** inherit the promises." (Hebrews 6:12 emphasis added). Notice we need faith and patience. Faith brings the inherited promise into manifestation but patience is also necessary because of the normal delay between the roots and the branches.

We need to actively fight doubt. Once we confirm something in the root we must be careful to guard against every evil thought that comes into our minds, because rest assured, this is warfare. During the battle, not only must we fight with thanksgiving, but we must also be careful to watch our words. We might say, "I'm in a mess. I sure hope God answers." That's not faith. That's hope. Instead, try saying something like, "I praise God He has answered in the root and I am rejoicing that in His timing He will manifest it in the branches." During this time we also need to be careful about who we share this with. Some people sow doubt with their words, though they mean well.

Finally, during the interim we need to be sure and keep our eyes on Jesus. Peter's mistake when he was walking on the water was he took his eyes off Jesus and looked at the waves and wind. And anytime we are waiting for the branches to manifest, the enemy will supply ample waves and wind to discourage us. The author to the Hebrews writes about, "fixing our eyes on Jesus, the author and perfecter of faith." (Hebrews 12:2). The word fix means to look away from one thing so as to see another. Be aware of the branches, but do not stare at their "non-withered" state. We must look to Jesus and His promise. Reality is what God's Word says, not what we perceive. If we hold on to that greater reality, we will see the answer manifest. The branches will wither.

7
God Has His Reasons

We don't like to wait. We want answers now. We may not say it out loud, but our attitude with God can be quite demanding. But we are not a peculiar generation. Those of the past felt the same way. King David wrote, "I am in distress; answer me quickly." (Psalm 69:17). He also penned these words: "In the day when I call answer me quickly." (Psalm 201:2). Both times he used the word quickly, which means "in a hurry, at once, soon, suddenly." The answer couldn't come soon enough for David, and we are just like him. It's not very long before we must face the frustrating reality that God is not in the same time zone as we are. He is not in a hurry. Instant manifestations are not the normal pattern.

When Jesus cursed the fig tree He intentionally delayed the manifestation of His word. There was no necessity for a gap in time, not with Him. Many of His miracles were instantaneous. Yet when specifically teaching a lesson on faith, he intentionally created a delay between when the word was given and its effects were seen. He wanted His disciples to understand they should expect a delay between the roots and the branches. I can think of at least five reasons God would allow a delay between His Word of promise and its manifestation in our lives.

1. The outworking of providence. Providence is the way God orchestrates all the events of the universe so everything ultimately fulfills His plans. The quintessential example of that is the birth of Christ. Paul wrote, "…when the fullness of the time came, God sent forth His Son, born of a woman, born under the Law…" (Galatians 4:4). Jesus came at just the right moment, but many things had to be orchestrated and lined up before He arrived. The first prophecy of His coming was early in Genesis. "And I will put enmity between you and the woman, and between your seed and her seed; He shall bruise you on the head, and you shall bruise him on the heel." (Genesis 3:15). It would take 4000 years from the time that prophecy was given, until the promise could be fulfilled. God had to call a man named Abram

from his home country of Ur and settle him as a family. It would take over 400 years for that family to grow into a nation. He had to raise up Moses and dictate to him the Law Israel was to live by; a document which served as the basis for conviction to enlighten His people to their awareness of the need for a savior. He moved nations until Rome came on the scene and established a universal language, which would make it possible for the good news of God's redemption to be spread throughout the ancient world. There was a universal peace (Pax Romana) and a universal road system that allowed the gospel to be carried to the ends of the known world.

He invested several thousands of years raising up prophets who would pen predictions of the coming Messiah. There were hundreds of details God put in place in preparation for the coming of His Son.

> The muscle of faith needs to be exercised and trials are one of the few means to do so. Mountains are opportunities to build faith.

That was all divine providence. Who knows how many details need to be worked out in our lives before the manifestation of God's answer can materialize in the branches? It could even be that God wants to change us first. When He offers the promise of a better future, the person you are now may not be adequate to handle the future He has in store. Between where you are now, and where He plans for you to be is a school of discipleship and refinement—all necessary preparation before the answer can manifest in the branches.

In fact, this may be part of the reason God allowed the mountain in your life in the first place. James writes, "Consider it all joy, my brethren, when you encounter various trials, knowing that the testing of your faith produces endurance. And let endurance have its perfect result, so that you may be perfect and complete, lacking in nothing." (James 1:2-4). Trials are allowed because they mature us.

The muscle of faith needs to be exercised and trials are one of the few means to do so. Mountains are opportunities to build faith. That's why James says to rejoice; not because we enjoy the trial, but because of the opportunity the trial provides. Trials produce endurance and James says in time we will be "complete, lacking nothing." (James 1:4). James doesn't mean we will be perfect, but we will be where God wants us to be. The delays God allows are part of the bigger picture, His program for conformity to the image of Christ (Romans 8:28-29). There is no other way for that to happen outside of the mountains in our lives.

2. God allows the delay to teach us to rely on His Word, rather than our senses. If the manifestation were immediate, then we would never trust the Word of God. The delay requires us to grab the promise of God's Word and hold onto it, but we would never need to hold on to the Word if the manifestation in the branches were immediate. We only learn to trust the word, when we learn to rely on that alone. When there is nothing left but the Word, when there is no evidence besides the Word, is that enough? When everything is saying, "No", can we trust God's "Yes"?

> The one thing that honors God more than anything else is when we trust His word. When we require proof from God, it brings Him down to our level.

This is important because it honors God. The one thing that honors God more than anything else is when we trust His word. When we require proof from God, it brings Him down to our level. We don't trust people unless there is proof, or a signature on the dotted line. But "God is not a man that He should lie." (Numbers 23:19). Jesus identified Himself as the truth (John 14:6). Satan, on the other hand, is "the father of lies." (John 8:44). God's Word is an expression of His character. He even describes the Son as the Word of God (John 1:1). So to doubt His Word is to doubt Him.

When Jesus encountered a Roman Centurion, He was asked to heal the soldier's servant. Jesus agreed and asked the Centurion to lead the way to his home. But the officer said he was not worthy to have Jesus come under his roof. Instead, he was confident that if Jesus just spoke the word his servant would be healed (Matthew 8:8-10). Jesus was blown away at the Centurion's faith, that he had such confidence in the mere word of Jesus. Jesus said to Thomas after seeing Him in His resurrected state, "Blessed are they who did not see, and yet believed." (John 20:29b).

Trust is at the foundation of intimacy and that is what God is interested in; that's what He gets from our relationship with Him. He can answer requests all day; it's nothing to Him. But what He wants is intimacy. Resting in His Word places us in the realm of the Spirit. Depending on our senses keeps us in the realm of the flesh. We cannot become intimate with God via the flesh. It is only through the spirit.

3. God allows the delay to teach us to keep Him as our priority, rather than the answer to our prayer. When we face a mountain what do we naturally care about more, God, or the mountain? In our flesh, it's the mountain, but God wants us to care more about Him. Shadrach, Meshach and Abednego had faith that God would deliver them from a fiery death, but even if He didn't they would still serve the Lord because their relationship with God was more important to them than His blessings. "If it be so, our God whom we serve is able to deliver us from the furnace of blazing fire; and He will deliver us out of your hand, O king. But even if He does not, let it be known to you, O king, that we are not going to serve your gods or worship the golden image that you have set up." (Daniel 3:17-18).

There is something unique about spending time with God in the interim. If I wait on Him during the interim as He teaches us to (thanking Him and praising Him in faith), it is the purest form of faith. In those moments we are expressing our trust in Him while still experiencing lack, while still facing the mountain. In that sense it becomes a true "sacrifice of praise to God, that is, the fruit of lips that give thanks to His name." (Hebrews 13:15b). This is very pleasing to God. The Psalmist cried, "My God, my God, why have You forsaken me? Far from my deliverance are the words of my groaning. O my God, I cry by day, but You do not answer; and by night, but I have no rest..." (Psalm 22:1-2). That was a man living in the gap. David was experiencing the tension between the promise of the root and the fulfillment in the branches. He acknowledged he was in the interim, and found it difficult. But then he continued with, "...yet You are holy, O You who are enthroned upon the praises of Israel." (Psalm 22:3). He acknowledged the holiness of God. Resident within that statement was the understanding that God is good, even though he felt God's silence. Praise in those moments can be given with the assurance that God sits enthroned on the praises of our hearts. If we spend the interim in praise and worship, God is exalted and comes near, even if we can't see, hear or feel Him.

> Sometimes God delays and allows the mountain to grow to an impossible size in order to show off His glory.

4. God allows the delay to heighten His glory. "Now a certain man was sick, Lazarus of Bethany, the village of Mary and her sister Martha. It was the Mary who anointed the Lord with ointment, and wiped His feet with her hair, whose brother Lazarus was sick. So the sisters sent word to Him, saying, 'Lord, behold, he whom You love is sick.'" (John 11:1-3). Word was sent to Jesus, but He intentionally stalled. Instead of traveling immediately to Bethany to heal His friend, Jesus delayed His trip, knowing that Lazarus would die. "Now Jesus loved Martha and her sister and Lazarus. So when He heard that he was sick, He then stayed two days longer in the place where He was." (John 11:5-6). Jesus knew His friend was now dead and told His disciples plainly that Lazarus had died (John 11:14). He intentionally let His friend die, when He had the power to heal him. When He finally arrived, the

sisters were upset, but Jesus had something better in mind than healing His friend's disease. Jesus raised him from the dead. That act, more than any other miracle Jesus did, elevated His glory. Many came to believe in Jesus because Lazarus, who had died and was buried, walked alive out of his own tomb after being dead for three days. No one could argue that Jesus raised him from the dead. His enemies could not dispute it, and so decided Jesus and Lazarus had to be put to death, and soon (John 11:51).

When God led Israel out of Egypt, He guided them to a dead end. The Red Sea was before them, two mountains were on either side of them and the Egyptian army was pressing in behind them. They had nowhere to go. There was no way out. Parting the Red Sea and providing a way of escape under those impossible conditions only served to heighten God's glory. Sometimes God delays and allows the mountain to grow to an impossible size in order to show off His glory.

During the interim, we have to wait on God. But waiting is not passive. It is active. Hebrews 6:12 says, "…that you will **not be sluggish**, but imitators of those who through faith and patience inherit the promises." (emphasis added). Sluggish means lazy. We do not wait for the promises like one who is lazy. We engage in active waiting. We wait with worship, giving God thanks and praise. We wait by quoting the Word, reciting the promise of God for our situation. We wait by rebuking the enemy, fighting off the doubt he will seek to hurl our way. We wait by serving others. When we think of waiting, don't picture someone reclining in an easy chair. Think of someone who waits on tables in a restaurant. We wait on the Lord in that manner by serving other people in His name. "Though youths grow weary and tired, and vigorous young men stumble badly, yet those who wait for the Lord will gain new strength; they will mount up with wings like eagles, they will run and not get tired, they will walk and not become weary." (Isaiah 40:30-31).

8
Silence In the Gap

Casting our mountains into the sea has everything to do with believing that what we pray is done in the root, and then we wait for it to manifest in the branches. But there are times when we pray and nothing happens in the root. Our prayers are ineffective. At certain times it's not an issue of waiting for the answer to manifest in the branches for the answer never came in the root in the first place. That happens sometimes and we need to understand why. There are a number of things we can do on our end that will render our prayers ineffective; that will keep anything from happening in the root.

Sometimes our prayers are ineffective because we hide sin in our hearts. "If I regard wickedness in my heart, the Lord will not hear; but certainly God has heard; He has given heed to the voice of my prayer. Blessed be God, Who has not turned away my prayer nor His lovingkindness from me." (Psalm 66:18-20). This passage is talking about God answering our prayers. The Psalmist says that God has heard him, so this is a person who has a righteous standing before God. However, he says that even though he has access to God, if he holds on to sin in his heart, God will not hear him. Sin causes a block in the heavenly pipeline.

This isn't only an Old Testament idea. On one occasion Jesus healed a man born blind. The Pharisees questioned the blind man about who healed him. They were angered that he said Jesus healed him. They accused Jesus of being a sinner. The man responded with devastating logic. He reminded them he had been born blind. Jesus healed him—a miracle that had never been performed in human history. That had to mean Jesus was clearly from God. Then the man said, "We know that God does not hear sinners; but if anyone is God-fearing and does His will, He hears him." (John 9:31). Jesus was heard because He is God-fearing, but notice the blind man said, "…God does not hear sinners…" (John 9:31).

We might be tempted to think if that's the case, then God is not going to hear any of our prayers because we all commit sin. We obviously stumble in many ways (James 3:2). But the kind of sin that keeps God from responding to us is unconfessed sin. When King David committed the infamous sin with Bathsheba he hid it for over a year. During that time, God's only message to David was that he needed to repent. David described the condition of his heart this way: "When I kept silent about my sin, my body wasted away through my groaning all day long. For day and night Your hand was heavy upon me; my vitality was drained away as with the fever heat of summer." (Psalm 32:3-4). The only thing God was willing to hear from David during that time was repentance. If there is hidden sin in our hearts, then that's the big issue in our relationship with God, not the mountain. In fact, sometimes God allows the mountain in our life specifically to deal with our sin.

Paul rebuked the Corinthian Christians because they were getting drunk at the Lord's Supper. God orchestrated some huge mountains in their lives specifically to get their attention about their sin.

> For, in the first place, when you come together as a church, I hear that divisions exist among you; and in part I believe it. For there must also be factions among you, so that those who are approved may become evident among you. Therefore when you meet together, it is not to eat the Lord's Supper, for in your eating each one takes his own supper first; and one is hungry and another is drunk. What! Do you not have houses in which to eat and drink? Or do you despise the church of God and shame those who have nothing? What shall I say to you? Shall I praise you? In this I will not praise you. For I received from the Lord that which I also delivered to you, that the Lord Jesus in the night in which He was betrayed took bread; and when He had given thanks, He broke it and said, "This is My body, which is for you; do this in remembrance of Me." In the same way He took the cup also after supper, saying, "This cup is the

new covenant in My blood; do this, as often as you drink it, in remembrance of Me." For as often as you eat this bread and drink the cup, you proclaim the Lord's death until He comes. Therefore whoever eats the bread or drinks the cup of the Lord in an unworthy manner, shall be guilty of the body and the blood of the Lord. But a man must examine himself, and in so doing he is to eat of the bread and drink of the cup. For he who eats and drinks, eats and drinks judgment to himself if he does not judge the body rightly. **For this reason many among you are weak and sick, and a number sleep.** (1 Corinthians 11:18-30 emphasis added).

When Israel went to battle against the city of Ai, they led with a small force, confident they could conquer the tiny city. But they were soundly defeated. Joshua inquired of the Lord why they had lost the battle. God revealed to Joshua that during the first battle against Jericho, in which Israel had been successful, someone in the army took some of the spoils of war for himself. God had instructed them prior to that first battle that all the spoils of that first city were for God. The Israelites were to touch nothing, but leave it for the Lord. Achan, came across some treasure during the battle and could not resist. He knew it was wrong for he dug a hole and hid the contraband under his tent. Once the sin was discovered, the spoils returned to God, and Achan punished, the army easily defeated Ai in battle. When the hidden sin was exposed and dealt with, there was victory. If we have hidden sin in our hearts, we must confess it and repent of it before God.

> Doubt can easily turn into unbelief. The enemy attacks us with doubt. We can't help that, but not allowing the doubt to form into unbelief is our responsibility.

Our prayers can be ineffective when we harbor doubt and unbelief. We have already dealt with doubt, so I won't expand too much on this, but there are a couple of things I want to emphasize. James makes it clear that continued doubt will hinder the manifestation of God's answer. "But he must ask in faith without any doubting, for the one who doubts is like the surf of the sea, driven and tossed by the wind. For that man ought not to expect that he will receive anything from the Lord, being a double-minded man, unstable in all his ways." (James 1:6-8). Doubt is a spiritual attack by the enemy and so we have to fight against it. Its greatest danger, however, is that doubt can easily turn into unbelief. The enemy attacks us with doubt. We can't help that, but not allowing the doubt to form into unbelief is our responsibility. We need to be clear about how doubt crystalizes into unbelief.

Israel, at first, was barred from entering into the Promised Land because of unbelief. The author to the book of Hebrews was admonishing the church of his day by referring back to the Israelites of old.

Therefore, just as the Holy Spirit says, "Today if you hear His voice, do not harden your hearts as when they provoked Me, as in the day of trial in the wilderness, where your fathers tried Me by testing Me, and saw My works for forty years. Therefore I was angry with this generation, and said, 'They always go astray in their heart, and they did not know My ways; as I swore in My wrath, They shall not enter My rest.'" (Hebrews 3:7-11).

Israel was barred from entering. They continually went astray and did not know God's ways. Later in the chapter, the Hebrew author summarizes the cause. "So we see that they were not able to enter because of unbelief." (Hebrews 3:19). Israel had an unbelief problem, but it began with doubt. The Bible makes clear what pushed it from doubt to unbelief. "For who provoked Him when they had heard? Indeed, did not all those who came out of Egypt led by Moses?" (Hebrews 3:16). The Israelites provoked God through their unbelief. The author gives us a clue to what he is speaking about specifically when he mentions the wilderness wanderings under Moses. The book of Numbers records the specific incident. "Then all the congregation lifted up their voices and cried, and the people wept that night. All the sons of Israel grumbled against Moses and Aaron; and the whole congregation said to them, 'Would that we had died in the land of Egypt! Or would that we had died in this wilderness!'" (Numbers 14:1-2).

> Grumbling and complaining causes doubt to morph into unbelief, and unbelief hinders God from acting on our behalf.

"The Lord said to Moses, 'How long will this people spurn Me? And how long will they not believe in Me, despite all the signs which I have performed in their midst? I will smite them with pestilence and dispossess them, and I will make you into a nation greater and mightier than they.'" (Numbers 14:11-12). Moses interceded for the people and God stayed His hand of judgment, but they were forced to wander in the wilderness another 38 years.

They provoked God because of their unbelief, but their unbelief was displayed by their complaining. Hear this, because it is so important; grumbling and complaining causes doubt to morph into unbelief, and unbelief hinders God from acting on our behalf.

Even Jesus was hindered by unbelief. "And He could do no miracle there except that He laid His hands on a few sick people and healed them. And He wondered at their unbelief." (Mark 6:5-6a). If our prayers are ineffective, it may be an issue of unbelief, evidenced by complaining.

Another issue that can cause our prayers to be ineffective is unforgiveness. It is insightful that when teaching about faith and the fig tree, Jesus intentionally referenced forgiveness. "Whenever you stand praying, forgive, if you have anything against anyone, so that your Father who is in heaven will also forgive you your transgressions." (Mark 11:25). When we refuse to forgive others it offends the Holy Spirit. "Do not grieve the Holy Spirit of God, by whom you were sealed for the day of redemption. Let all bitterness and wrath and anger and clamor and slander be put away from you, along with all malice. Be kind to one another, tender-hearted, forgiving each other, just as God in Christ also has forgiven you." (Ephesians 4:30-32). The key issue here is that Christ has forgiven us. Those who have truly received grace understand they need to extend it to others.

> Those who have truly been forgiven by God and understand the grace of undeserved redemption are compelled to extend the same to others.

Jesus told a story about a man who owed a king an enormous sum of money. The king graciously forgave the man's debt. The man later found a peer who owed him an insignificant amount. He refused to forgive the debt. When the king heard of it, he was outraged. "Then summoning him, his lord said to him, 'You wicked slave, I forgave you all that debt because you entreated me. Should you not also have had mercy on your fellow slave, even as I had mercy on you?'" (Matthew 18:32-33). Our problem is that we often lose sight of the bigger picture. We are so focused on the pain and loss suffered at the hands of another, that we forget the enormous debt God forgave.

When confronted with an offense, we must choose to keep our eyes focused on the cross. The issue in forgiveness is not the size of the other person's offense, but the depth of Christ's sacrifice. We sometimes struggle with forgiveness because it seems that if we release the other person, an injustice will be done. If we choose to assume the loss, then they have gotten away with a "crime" and there is no sense of justice. Exactly! God forbid if He were to take the same approach with us!

There is nothing fair in salvation. We do not deserve it. Jesus did not deserve to suffer on the cross in our place. It is not fair that He had to assume the loss on our behalf, but I am glad He did. The debt He paid for you and me is eternal. How can that compare with the offense someone leveled against us? If we claim forgiveness from God, but refuse to extend mercy to others, we expose our hypocrisy and show that we really have never understood the grace of God. Those who have truly been forgiven by God and understand the grace of undeserved redemption are compelled to extend the same to others. When I consider the depth of my own sin and the magnitude of God's mercy, who am I to withhold that from others?

When we withhold forgiveness it harms other relationships in our lives. The author to the book of Hebrews talks about a root of bitterness that brings harm to others. "Pursue peace with all men, and the sanctification without which no one will see the Lord. See to it that no one comes short of the grace of God; that no root of bitterness springing up causes trouble, and by it many be defiled;" (Hebrews 12:14-15). That verse identifies bitterness as a root. We think of roots being hidden underground. Sometimes, however, the roots are exposed. Have you ever been under the shade of an old tree where the soil had eroded enough that the uppermost roots were exposed? The author says that sometimes those roots spring up, they break the surface of the soil. When they do, they cause trouble. The word for trouble means, "to afflict" or "cause to suffer".[7] When there is a root of bitterness in someone's heart, the person who is troubled the most is the one holding on to unforgiveness. It eats away at their soul like a cancer.

Eventually, however, that poisonous root springs up and defiles other relationships. When I was a student at Asbury College I worked for a brief time as a short order cook in the student center. One night I was left to clean up the grill. I had never done it before and was not given any instructions other than sweep, mop and throw away the trash. I scraped off the grill and did not know what to do with the hot grease. There was a large bucket containing some soapy water standing in the corner. It seemed like a good idea to me to pour the grease in the bucket of water. Bad decision! When the grease made contact with the water, it reminded me of one of those science experiments where you make a volcano. Everything started reacting. I didn't pour that much grease into the bucket, but it bubbled over into a constant lava flow. It seemed there was an endless supply of grease. It continued to bubble over until the entire back room was covered in a layer of greasy water. The reaction of the water to the grease was totally disproportionate to the amount of grease I poured in the bucket.

When someone holds bitterness in his or her heart, any slight offense from another person is like pouring hot grease into a bucket of water. The reaction of the person is often disproportionate to the offense. Innocent people become the focus of their anger. They end up sabotaging relationships in their life because of a previous hurt.

Unforgiveness opens the door to Satan's attack in our lives. The Apostle Paul rebuked the Corinthian church because they ignored a blatant sin in the church. Evidently, the church took action because in his second letter to them, he admonished them to forgive the brother once he repented of his sin. "But one whom you forgive anything, I forgive also; for indeed what I have forgiven, if I have forgiven anything, I did it for your sakes in the presence of Christ, so that no advantage would be taken of us by Satan, for we are not ignorant of his schemes." (2Corinthians 2:10-11). Notice that Paul warned them that if they did not forgive the brother, Satan would take advantage of them. Apparently, unforgiveness gives him a foothold in the church.

Paul understood that Satan was waiting to exploit the church through their unforgiveness. If he can bait us into it, it gives him an advantage in our lives. "Be angry, and yet do not sin; do not let the sun go down on your anger, and do not give the devil an opportunity." (Ephesians 4:26-27). To hold on to our anger means we are not forgiving, and that gives the devil an opportunity to exploit our life. When we don't deal with our anger appropriately, it goes under ground. That gives the enemy a base of operations from which to work in our hearts. This is an effective trap. If we take hold of offense, then God will not heed our prayers. That breaks down the hedge of protection in our lives and leaves us vulnerable against Satan's attacks.

People often become frustrated with forgiveness because they have the wrong idea about what it means. Let's start by being clear about what forgiveness is not. Forgiveness is not saying that what the person did to us is all right. It is not okay what they did. If you were offended or hurt, that pain is real. What that person did to you is not fair.

Forgiveness is also not sweeping the offense under the carpet. We don't pretend the incident never happened. It did happen and it cheapens the act of grace to pretend it did not.

Forgiveness is not forgetting what happened. That is a human impossibility. We can suppress the memory, but how much better to heal the memory.

Forgiveness is not an emotion. It is not about making self feel a certain way about someone. Rather, it is a choice of the will.

To forgive does not mean we have to tolerate continued abuse or injury. God is not calling us to be doormats that people can walk over. That is really an issue of trust, which is different from forgiveness. Forgiveness is unearned and unconditional. It is a gift of grace. Trust must be earned.

Forgiveness is not offered with conditions. We don't say, "I'll forgive you if you're truly sorry", or "if you admit your guilt", or "if you ask for my forgiveness".

What then is forgiveness? Webster's Dictionary says forgiveness is "to give up resentment against; to let go of the desire to punish, to pardon, to cancel or remit a debt".[8] The English word comes from two Latin words meaning, "to give" and "thoroughly".[9] It makes it clear that we are to give wholeheartedly. Jesus concluded the story of the unforgiving man with these words. "My heavenly Father will also do the same to you, if each of you does not forgive his brother from your heart." (Matthew 18:35). He added that it had to be from the heart, not just something we say with our mouth. It's giving thoroughly. The Greek word means "to send away"[10], to let it alone. It means to drop it. We are to do that with our whole heart.

It is a choice of the will. When I lead people to forgive others, I am careful about how they word their prayer. Often they will begin to pray something like this. "Lord, please help me to feel forgiveness in my heart toward…" I gently stop them and tell them that it isn't something God will do for us, but something we must make a choice with our will to do and then God will empower our choice of obedience. In addition, it isn't a feeling, but a decision that will in time affect our feelings. When they start back into the prayer, I have them pray, "Father, in obedience to your Word, I choose with my will to forgive…"

> Choosing to forgive, even when we do not feel like it, is not hypocritical. It is rather, a responsible first step to eventually changing how we feel.

To forgive means that I release my right to condemn the offender. When an offense is committed someone has to assume the loss. For example, if a guest came to my home and broke a vase, someone would have to pay for it. The host might assure the guest they need not worry and that they do not need to pay for the vase. That is a gracious act on the part of the host. The vase, however, must be replaced and the host is making the choice to assume the cost. That is what forgiveness is. We make the choice to absorb the cost.

Forgiveness means we transfer our legal right of judgment over to God. When someone hurts us we have a legal claim over him or her. They have committed a sin against us. When we forgive, we release that sin and give the judgment to the Lord. Stephen prayed that way while being stoned. Acts 7 tells us that he prayed the sins of his persecutors would not be held against them. He had the right to pray that because he was the offended party. That is a powerful tool in the realm of the Spirit to use when offended. We can pray for their good, which then leaves room for God to work in their life to bring about His will in them (Romans 12:14-21).

One issue that hinders forgiveness is the problem of our feelings. People will try to pray to forgive others, but do not feel kindly toward that person. I have heard people protest, "Even if I say the words, I will feel hatred and so I am a hypocrite". It is right here that we need to understand the interplay between the will, mind and emotion. I said forgiveness is a choice of the will. It is not an emotion. That is a vital truth. If we miss that we can be frustrated and discouraged in our attempt to feel forgiving toward another. God commands us to forgive, but if it is a matter of my emotions, how can I choose how I am going to feel? I can't. We have no direct control over our emotions. Unless you are an actor, emotions are not things we can turn on and off. We do have control over what we choose to dwell on, and our thoughts have a direct effect on our emotional state.

In an interview from *Guideposts Magazine*, Corrie ten Boom, Holocaust survivor and author, told of not being able to forget a wrong that had been done to her. She had forgiven the person, but she kept rehashing the incident and so couldn't sleep. She writes of her eventual release from the feelings of unforgiveness. "His help came in the form of a kindly Lutheran pastor to whom I confessed my failure after two sleepless weeks. 'Up in the church tower', he said, nodding out the window, 'is a bell which is rung by pulling on a rope. But you know what. After the sexton lets go of the rope, the bell keeps on swinging. First ding, then dong. Slower and slower until there's a final dong and it stops. I believe the same thing is true of forgiveness. When we forgive, we take our hand off the rope. But if we've been tugging at our grievances for a long time, we mustn't be surprised if the old angry thoughts keep coming for a while. They're just the ding-dongs of the old bell slowing down.' And so it proved to be. There were a few more midnight reverberations, a couple of dings when the subject came up in my conversations, but the force—which was my willingness in the matter—had gone out of them. They came less and less often and at the last stopped altogether: we can trust God not only above our emotions, but also above our thoughts."[11] Choosing to forgive, even when we do not feel like it, is not hypocritical. It is rather, a responsible first step to eventually changing how we feel.

Another barrier to forgiveness is memory. We might object, "Even if I say the words I will still remember what they did. I can never forget it." God does not call us to forget the offense. He does not forget the sins we have committed against Him. That might sound like a contradiction, because Scripture seems to indicate that He does indeed forget. "I, even I, am the one who wipes out your transgressions for My own sake; and I will not remember your sins." (Isaiah 43:25). "For I will be merciful to their iniquities, and I will remember their sins no more." (Hebrews 8:12). "And their sins and their lawless deeds I will remember no more." (Hebrews 10:17). These passages seem to say God remembers our sin no more. Does God literally forget our sins? Is it possible for Him to so forget our sins that He cannot recall them in His mind? Do you remember the sins you have committed in the past? If God forgot them, but you remembered them, that would mean you possessed

> When we forgive, someone is released from prison. To our delight, we discover that person is us.

knowledge God did not. Can God forget so that He lacks knowledge that we possess? That would mean God was not omniscient. How do we reconcile the apparent contradiction?

What the Scripture means, is that God will not remember our sins against us. The Psalmist expressed the idea when he wrote, "Do not remember the iniquities of our forefathers against us." (Psalm 79:8a). We may not mentally forget with our brain, but we can choose not to remember the offense against them anymore. How? We do so by choosing not to use the memory of the offense against the other person. We choose not to talk against the other person to others. We choose not to dwell on the offense. We choose to remind ourselves that we have forgiven the person.

When I lead people to pray to forgive, I have them write down the names of their offenders and their offenses. I make sure they understand the issues just mentioned in this chapter. They then begin by praising God for the cross and His work of forgiveness in their lives. I have them focus on their own debt of sin and God's grace and mercy toward them. Then I instruct them to take the first name and lift it before the Lord. I encourage them to pray words similar to the following: "Lord, I choose in obedience to Your Word, to forgive so and so for…" Then they finish the sentence by listing the offenses against them. I then ask them to intercede for the person, asking God to forgive the offender. Once they are finished praying over the list, I have them destroy it as a testimony of God's promise of new beginnings. I remind them that their forgiveness will most likely not effect a change in the offender. I do, however, encourage the individual to expect major changes in themselves as God works powerfully in their lives to set them free. When we forgive, someone is released from prison. To our delight, we discover that person is us.

If we have a mountain in our life that isn't moving, perhaps the blockage is one of these things I have mentioned. God doesn't stand over us with condemnation (Romans 8:1), but He will bring conviction to our hearts; an inner knowing that this is a problem that needs to be dealt with.

The Mysteries Of The Interim

Sometimes we pray God's will as far as we know. We pray with pure motivations, and we make sure all is well between God, and us. But God's answer is still, "No". When that happens we can't help but wonder why. It is at that point that we have to peer behind the curtain into the mysterious ways of God. "'For My thoughts are not your thoughts, nor are your ways My ways,' declares the Lord. 'For as the heavens are higher than the earth, so are My ways higher than your ways and My thoughts than your thoughts.'" (Isaiah 55:8-9). Some people may reference this verse as a cop out. Things don't work out as they want so they resign themselves to God's ways being beyond ours, shrugging it off as if it were some kind of divine fate. That is not how I am thinking of this verse. When we face a mountain, we need to pray diligently, but there will be times when the answer doesn't come and we have no explanation. At those times we may never know the specific reason, but we can learn some things about the mysterious ways of God that will help when that happens.

First, we need to know that God is not capricious or fickle. The gods of mythology had mood swings like the changing direction of the wind. Their superstitious followers never knew if their actions would please or offend them. They lived in uncertainty and fear. The Bible presents the true God very differently. James speaks of God as having "no variation or shifting shadow." (James 1:17). Malachi says, "For I, the Lord, do not change." (Malachi 3:6). Hebrews says, "Jesus Christ is the same yesterday and today and forever." (Hebrews 13:8). That means God does not get in a bad mood, or decide things on a whim. He always has a reason for what He does, even though we may never know it. Scripture does, however, offer some reasons for God's no.

Sometimes God says no for the sake of our spiritual health. "To keep me from exalting myself, there was given me a thorn in the flesh, a messenger of Satan to torment me—to keep me from exalting myself! Concerning this I implored the Lord three times that it might leave me. And He has said to me, 'My grace is sufficient for you, for power is perfected in weakness.' Most gladly, therefore, I will rather boast about my weaknesses, so that the power of Christ may dwell in me." (2 Corinthians 7b-9). Paul was suffering from something he described as a thorn, and even said it was tormenting him. Not only that, but it was specifically from Satan. That certainly sounds like something God would not want in our lives. Paul implored God to remove it three different times, but God still said no. He had a bigger purpose in mind. The first half of verse seven says it was, "...to keep me from exalting myself..." (2 Corinthians 12:7a). Paul's heavenly experience was apparently unlike any other (2 Corinthians 12:2-4). To be privileged to see what he did was unprecedented. God kept Satan on a leash, but used him to keep Paul from arrogance.

Sometimes God says no because of our personal calling. The desire of David's heart was to build a temple to God, but God told him no.

> David said to Solomon, "My son, I had intended to build a house to the name of the Lord my God. But the word of the Lord came to me, saying, 'You have shed much blood and have waged great wars; you shall not build a house to My name, because you have shed so much blood on the earth before Me. Behold, a son will be born to you, who shall be a man of rest; and I will give him rest from all his enemies on every side; for his name shall be Solomon, and I will give peace and quiet to Israel in his days. He shall build a house for My name, and he shall be My son and I will be his father; and I will establish the throne of his kingdom over Israel forever.'" (1 Chronicles 22:7-10).

David was denied the privilege of building the temple, because he was a warrior. Yet, it was God who called him to be a warrior. When David fought the Philistines, he was following God's call. God needed David to function in the role of a soldier, which exempted him from building the temple. In David's case kingdom needs trumped personal desires. We each have a unique calling from God (1 Corinthians 12:11). God never second guesses the role He calls us to take. "For God's gifts and His call are irrevocable. [He never withdraws them when once they are given, and He does not change His mind about those to whom He gives His grace or to whom He sends His call.]" (Romans 11:29 Amplified Bible). Sometimes God's calling on our life requires Him to say no to a personal request because He has another purpose in mind for us.

Sometimes God says no because of Kingdom expansion. Paul wanted to travel into Asia and take the gospel there, but God had other plans. He redirected Paul in a vision.

They passed through the Phrygian and Galatian region, having been forbidden by the Holy Spirit to speak the word in Asia; and after they came to Mysia, they were trying to go into Bithynia, and the Spirit of Jesus did not permit them; and passing by Mysia, they came down to Troas. A vision appeared to Paul in the night: a man of Macedonia was standing and appealing to him, and saying, "Come over to Macedonia and help us." When he had seen the vision, immediately we sought to go into Macedonia, concluding that God had called us to preach the gospel to them. (Acts 16:6-10).

God wanted the gospel to reach the shores of Europe. It was that shift in focus that opened the gospel up to the entire world and allowed it eventually to reach across the globe into every nation and tribe. God may deny us, because our investment in His Kingdom is larger than our personal desire.

Sometimes God says no and the reason is kept from us. Sometimes His refusal or silence in the face of our persistent petitions doesn't fit into any categories. We just don't know why. We know He must have a reason, but we are not told what it is. That seems to be the hardest to handle. In those times we have to come to peace with not knowing why, but even then, there are some things we can know.

Even in the face of mystery, God promises His grace. "And He has said to me, 'My grace is sufficient for you, for power is perfected in weakness.' Most gladly, therefore, I will rather boast about my weaknesses, so that the power of Christ may dwell in me." (2 Corinthians 12:9). Grace is the presence of God coming into our lives to empower us to be and do what He calls us to be and do. We may never know the why, but we can always know the *Who*—who it is that will empower us to face our mountain. In the face of mystery, God also promises His presence.

In those times when the answer does not come, when there is no confirmation in our spirit that God has answered in the root, what do we do? First, we fight the fight of faith. Even Paul prayed intensely on three occasions over his thorn. Only then did he learn God's answer was no. So we pray with persistence and expectation. We make sure our wills are aligned with God's will. And if the answer is still no, we trust God, because no matter how He answers, no matter how mysterious His ways, no matter how confusing or distant or silent He seems, know this: God is good, and God is love.

I have found that those occasions when God is silent and we have no answers to deal with our mountain are rare. If we take the time to search the Scriptures and discern the will of God; if we pray until our spirits discern God's yes in the root; if we thank Him with expectation that His answer will manifest in the branches, we will see the wonders of God unfold in our lives. My prayer for you is that as you learn to apply Jesus' teaching to your life, you will see mountain after mountain taken up and cast into the sea to the glory of God.

NOTES:

[1] Alfred Jones, *Jones' Dictionary of Old Testament Proper Names* (Grand Rapids, MI: Kregel Publications, 1990) :315

[2] Warren Baker, D.R.E., General Editor, *The Complete Word Study Old Testament* (Chattanooga, TN, AMG Publishers, 1994)

[3] Bob George, *Classic Christianity: Life's Too Short To Miss the Real Thing.* (Eugene, OR, Harvest House Publishers, 1989)

[4] James Strong, S.T.D., LL.D. *The Exhaustive Concordance of the Bible.* (Nashville TN, Abingdon, 1980)

[5] George Muller. Org. Quotes. Posted July 27, 2017. http://www.georgemuller.org/quotes/category/faith

[6] Brainyquote.com https://www.brainyquote.com/quotes/quotes/l/ludwigvanb1530 98.html

[7] W.E. Vine and Merrill F. Unger, William White, Jr., *Vine's Complete Expository Dictionary of Old and New Testament Words* (Nashville, TN: Thomas Nelson Publishers, 1996) : 644

[8] Noah Webster, *Webster's New Twentieth Century Dictionary of the English Language*, 2nd Ed. (New York, NY: The World Publishing Company, 1961)

[9] John Ayto, *Dictionary of Word Origins* (New York, NY: Arcade Publishing, 1990) :236

[10] W.E. Vine and Merrill F. Unger, William White, Jr., *Vine's Complete Expository Dictionary of Old and New Testament Words* (Nashville, TN: Thomas Nelson Publishers, 1996) : 250

[11] Guideposts Classics:Corrie ten Boom on Forgiveness. Posted July 24, 2014. Accessed August 2017. https://www.guideposts.org/better-living/positive-living/guideposts-classics-corrie-ten-boom-on-forgiveness.